Cram101 Textbook Outlines to accompany:

International Organizations: Principles and Issues

Bennett and Oliver, 7th Edition

An Academic Internet Publishers (AIPI) publication (c) 2007.

Cram101 and Cram101.com are AIPI publications and services. All notes, highlights, reviews, and practice tests are prepared by AIPI for use in AIPI publications, all rights reserved.

You have a discounted membership at www.Cram101.com with this book.

Get all of the practice tests for the chapters of this textbook, and access in-depth reference material for writing essays and papers. Here is an example from a Cram101 Biology text:

When you need problem solving help with math, stats, and other disciplines, www.Cram101.com will walk through the formulas and solutions step by step.

With Cram101.com online, you also have access to extensive reference material.

You will nail those essays and papers. Here is an example from a Cram101 Biology text:

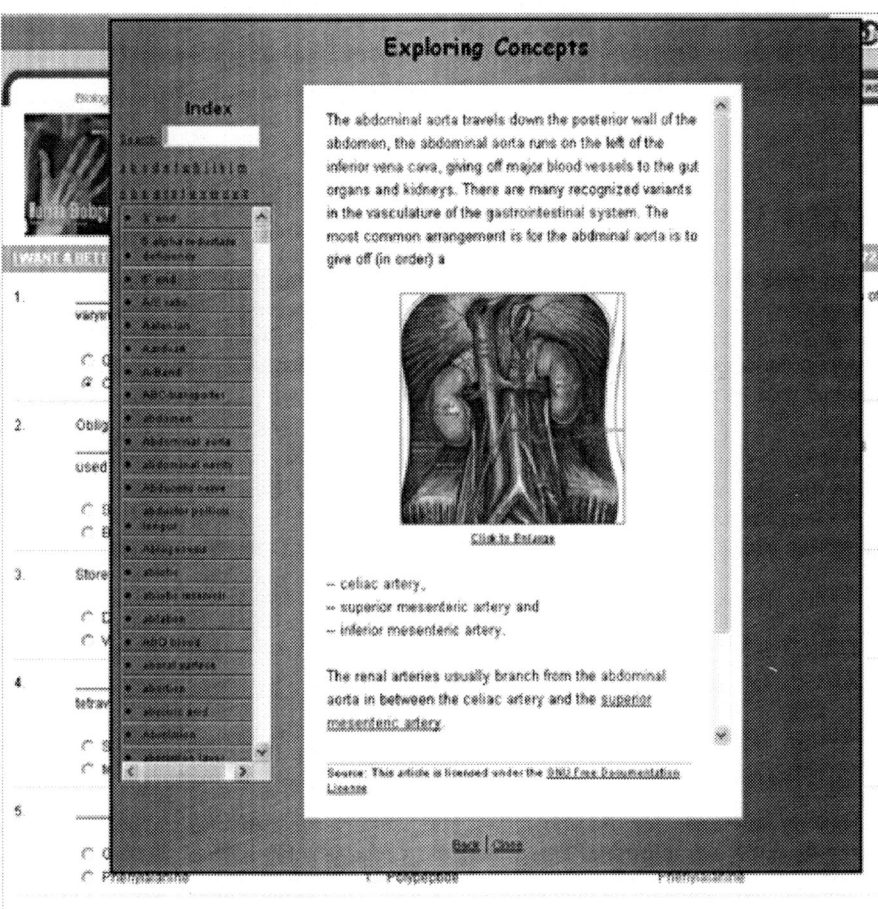

Visit **www.Cram101.com**, click Sign Up at the top of the screen, and enter DK73DW in the promo code box on the registration screen. Access to www.Cram101.com is normally $9.95, but because you have purchased this book, your access fee is only $4.95. Sign up and stop highlighting textbooks forever.

Learning System

Cram101 Textbook Outlines is a learning system. The notes in this book are the highlights of your textbook, you will never have to highlight a book again.

How to use this book. Take this book to class, it is your notebook for the lecture. The notes and highlights on the left hand side of the pages follow the outline and order of the textbook. All you have to do is follow along while your intructor presents the lecture. Circle the items emphasized in class and add other important information on the right side. With Cram101 Textbook Outlines you'll spend less time writing and more time listening. Learning becomes more efficient.

Cram101.com Online

Increase your studying efficiency by using Cram101.com's practice tests and online reference material. It is the perfect complement to Cram101 Textbook Outlines. Use self-teaching matching tests or simulate in-class testing with comprehensive multiple choice tests, or simply use Cram's true and false tests for quick review. Cram101.com even allows you to enter your in-class notes for an integrated studying format combining the textbook notes with your class notes.

Visit **www.Cram101.com**, click Sign Up at the top of the screen, and enter **DK73DW715** in the promo code box on the registration screen. Access to www.Cram101.com is normally $9.95, but because you have purchased this book, your access fee is only $4.95. Sign up and stop highlighting textbooks forever.

Copyright © 2007 by Academic Internet Publishers, Inc. All rights reserved. "Cram101"® and "Never Highlight a Book Again!"® are registered trademarks of Academic Internet Publishers, Inc. The Cram101 Textbook Outline series is printed in the United States. ISBN: 1-4288-0723-3

International Organizations: Principles and Issues
Bennett and Oliver, 7th

CONTENTS

1. INTRODUCTION 2
2. A GREAT EXPERIMENT: THE LEAGUE OF NATIONS 16
3. THE GENESIS OF THE UNITED NATIONS 26
4. BASIC PRINCIPLES AND ORGANIZATION OF THE UNITED NATIONS 34
5. BASIC STRUCTURE AND OPERATIONS OF THE UNITED NATIONS 44
6. PEACEFUL SETTLEMENT OF DISPUTES 54
7. COLLECTIVE SECURITY AND ITS ALTERNATIVES: THEORY AND PRACTICE 66
8. THE SEARCH FOR JUSTICE UNDER LAW 76
9. CONTROLLING THE INSTRUMENTS OF WAR 90
10. VARIETIES OF REGIONALISM 102
11. GLOBALIZATION, TRANSNATIONALISM, AND INTERNATIONAL ORGANIZATION 122
12. PROMOTING ECONOMIC WELFARE 138
13. MANAGING GLOBAL RESOURCES 162
14. PROMOTING SOCIAL PROGRESS 176
15. HUMAN RIGHTS AND THE STRUGGLE FOR SELF-GOVERNMENT 188
16. INTERNATIONAL ADMINISTRATION AND THE SEARCH FOR LEADERSHIP 200
17. INTERNATIONAL ORGANIZATION IN RETROSPECT AND PROSPECT 214

Chapter 1. INTRODUCTION

Affirm	To confirm or uphold a former judgment or order of a court is to affirm. Appellate courts, for instance, may affirm the decisions of lower courts.
United Nations	An international organization created by multilateral treaty in 1945 to promote social and economic cooperation among nations and to protect human rights is the United Nations.
Interdependence	The extent to which departments depend on each other for resources or materials to accomplish their tasks is referred to as interdependence.
Transnational	Transnational focuses on the heightened interconnectivity between people all around the world and the loosening of boundaries between countries.
Sovereignty	A country or region's power and ability to rule itself and manage its own affairs. Some feel that membership in international organizations such as the WTO is a threat to their sovereignty.
Instrument	Instrument refers to an economic variable that is controlled by policy makers and can be used to influence other variables, called targets. Examples are monetary and fiscal policies used to achieve external and internal balance.
Operation	A standardized method or technique that is performed repetitively, often on different materials resulting in different finished goods is called an operation.
Analyst	Analyst refers to a person or tool with a primary function of information analysis, generally with a more limited, practical and short term set of goals than a researcher.
Grievance	A charge by employees that management is not abiding by the terms of the negotiated labormanagement agreement is the grievance.
Interest	In finance and economics, interest is the price paid by a borrower for the use of a lender's money. In other words, interest is the amount of paid to "rent" money for a period of time.
Accommodation	Accommodation is a term used to describe a delivery of nonconforming goods meant as a partial performance of a contract for the sale of goods, where a full performance is not possible.
Compromise	Compromise occurs when the interaction is moderately important to meeting goals and the goals are neither completely compatible nor completely incompatible.
Channel	Channel, in communications (sometimes called communications channel), refers to the medium used to convey information from a sender (or transmitter) to a receiver.
Points	Loan origination fees that may be deductible as interest by a buyer of property. A seller of property who pays points reduces the selling price by the amount of the points paid for the buyer.
Coercion	Economic coercion is when an agent puts economic pressure onto the victim. The most common example of this is cutting off the supply to an essential resource, such as water.
Charter	Charter refers to an instrument or authority from the sovereign power bestowing the right or power to do business under the corporate form of organization. Also, the organic law of a city or town, and representing a portion of the statute law of the state.
Trend	Trend refers to the long-term movement of an economic variable, such as its average rate of increase or decrease over enough years to encompass several business cycles.
Regulation	Regulation refers to restrictions state and federal laws place on business with regard to the conduct of its activities.
Policy	Similar to a script in that a policy can be a less than completely rational decision-making method. Involves the use of a pre-existing set of decision steps for any problem that presents itself.
In kind	Referring to a payment made with goods instead of money is an in kind. An expression relating to the insurer's right in many Property contracts to replace damaged objects with new or equivalent (in kind) material, rather than to pay a cash benefit.

Chapter 1. INTRODUCTION

Chapter 1. INTRODUCTION

Management	Management characterizes the process of leading and directing all or part of an organization, often a business, through the deployment and manipulation of resources. Early twentieth-century management writer Mary Parker Follett defined management as "the art of getting things done through people."
Firm	An organization that employs resources to produce a good or service for profit and owns and operates one or more plants is referred to as a firm.
Consolidation	The combination of two or more firms, generally of equal size and market power, to form an entirely new entity is a consolidation.
Cosmopolitanism	Cosmopolitanism is the idea that all of humanity belongs to a single moral community. This is contrasted with ideologies of patriotism and nationalism. Cosmopolitanism may or may not entail some sort of world government or it may simply refer to more inclusive moral, economic, and/or political relationships between nations or individuals of different nations.
Authority	Authority in agency law, refers to an agent's ability to affect his principal's legal relations with third parties. Also used to refer to an actor's legal power or ability to do something. In addition, sometimes used to refer to a statute, case, or other legal source that justifies a particular result.
Service	Service refers to a "non tangible product" that is not embodied in a physical good and that typically effects some change in another product, person, or institution. Contrasts with good.
Free trade	Free trade refers to a situation in which there are no artificial barriers to trade, such as tariffs and quotas. Usually used, often only implicitly, with frictionless trade, so that it implies that there are no barriers to trade of any kind.
International law	Law that governs affairs between nations and that regulates transactions between individuals and businesses of different countries is an international law.
Comprehensive	A comprehensive refers to a layout accurate in size, color, scheme, and other necessary details to show how a final ad will look. For presentation only, never for reproduction.
De jure	According to the law is called de jure. Practices may exist de jure and not be obeyed or observed by the people.
Emancipation	Emancipation is the act of freeing or being freed/the relinquishment of control; its meaning encompasses both being able to be as one is (or as a political group chooses to be) without having to adjust to another power, while simultaneously being a contributing part or party to the whole.
Imperialism	Imperialism is a policy of extending control or authority over foreign entities as a means of acquisition and/or maintenance of empires. This is either through direct territorial conquest or settlement, or through indirect methods of exerting control on the politics and/or economy of these other entities. The term is often used to describe the policy of a nation's dominance over distant lands, regardless of whether the nation considers itself part of the empire.
Principal	In agency law, one under whose direction an agent acts and for whose benefit that agent acts is a principal.
Leadership	Management merely consists of leadership applied to business situations; or in other words: management forms a sub-set of the broader process of leadership.
Cooperative	A business owned and controlled by the people who use it, producers, consumers, or workers with similar needs who pool their resources for mutual gain is called cooperative.
Supply	Supply is the aggregate amount of any material good that can be called into being at a certain price point; it comprises one half of the equation of supply and demand. In classical economic theory, a curve representing supply is one of the factors that produce price.
Arbitration	Arbitration is a form of mediation or conciliation, where the mediating party is given power by the disputant parties to settle the dispute by making a finding. In practice arbitration is generally used as a substitute for judicial systems, particularly when the judicial processes are viewed as too slow,

Chapter 1. INTRODUCTION

Chapter 1. INTRODUCTION

	expensive or biased. Arbitration is also used by communities which lack formal law, as a substitute for formal law.
Appeal	Appeal refers to the act of asking an appellate court to overturn a decision after the trial court's final judgment has been entered.
Promotion	Promotion refers to all the techniques sellers use to motivate people to buy products or services. An attempt by marketers to inform people about products and to persuade them to participate in an exchange.
Standardization	Standardization, in the context related to technologies and industries, is the process of establishing a technical standard among competing entities in a market, where this will bring benefits without hurting competition.
Exchange	The trade of things of value between buyer and seller so that each is better off after the trade is called the exchange.
Commercial law	The law that relates to the rights of property and persons engaged in trade or commerce and regulates corporate contracts, hiring practices, and the manufacture and sales of consumer goods is called commercial law.
Balance	In banking and accountancy, the outstanding balance is the amount of money owned, (or due), that remains in a deposit account (or a loan account) at a given date, after all past remittances, payments and withdrawal have been accounted for. It can be positive (then, in the balance sheet of a firm, it is an asset) or negative (a liability).
Standing	Standing refers to the legal requirement that anyone seeking to challenge a particular action in court must demonstrate that such action substantially affects his legitimate interests before he will be entitled to bring suit.
Treaties	The first source of international law, consisting of agreements or contracts between two or more nations that are formally signed by an authorized representative and ratified by the supreme power of each nation are called treaties.
Equity	Equity is the name given to the set of legal principles, in countries following the English common law tradition, which supplement strict rules of law where their application would operate harshly, so as to achieve what is sometimes referred to as "natural justice."
Technology	The body of knowledge and techniques that can be used to combine economic resources to produce goods and services is called technology.
Coalition	An informal alliance among managers who support a specific goal is called coalition.
Ad hoc	Ad hoc is a Latin phrase which means "for this purpose." It generally signifies a solution that has been tailored to a specific purpose and is makeshift and non-general, such as a handcrafted network protocol or a specific-purpose equation, as opposed to general solutions.
Security	Security refers to a claim on the borrower future income that is sold by the borrower to the lender. A security is a type of transferable interest representing financial value.
Commerce	Commerce is the exchange of something of value between two entities. It is the central mechanism from which capitalism is derived.
Functional organization	Functional organization is a method of organization in which chapters and sections of a manual correspond to business functions, not specific departments or work groups.
Conflict resolution	Conflict resolution is the process of resolving a dispute or a conflict. Successful conflict resolution occurs by providing each side's needs, and adequately addressing their interests so that they are each satisfied with the outcome. Conflict resolution aims to end conflicts before they start or lead to physical fighting.

Go to **Cram101.com** for the Practice Tests for this Chapter.

Chapter 1. INTRODUCTION

Chapter 1. INTRODUCTION

Committee	A long-lasting, sometimes permanent team in the organization structure created to deal with tasks that recur regularly is the committee.
Mediation	Mediation consists of a process of alternative dispute resolution in which a (generally) neutral third party using appropriate techniques, assists two or more parties to help them negotiate an agreement, with concrete effects, on a matter of common interest.
Prerogative	Prerogative refers to a special power, privilege, or immunity, usually used in reference to an official or his office.
Economic interdependence	Economic interdependence describes countries/nation-states and/or supranational states such as the European Union (EU) or North American Free Trade Agreement (NAFTA) that are interdependent for any (or all) of the following: food, energy, minerals, manufactured goods, multinational/transnational corporations, financial institutions and foreign debt.
Depression	Depression refers to a prolonged period characterized by high unemployment, low output and investment, depressed business confidence, falling prices, and widespread business failures. A milder form of business downturn is a recession.
Economy	The income, expenditures, and resources that affect the cost of running a business and household are called an economy.
Administration	Administration refers to the management and direction of the affairs of governments and institutions; a collective term for all policymaking officials of a government; the execution and implementation of public policy.
Social responsibility	Social responsibility is a doctrine that claims that an entity whether it is state, government, corporation, organization or individual has a responsibility to society.
Diffusion	Diffusion is the process by which a new idea or new product is accepted by the market. The rate of diffusion is the speed that the new idea spreads from one consumer to the next.
Loyalty	Marketers tend to define customer loyalty as making repeat purchases. Some argue that it should be defined attitudinally as a strongly positive feeling about the brand.
International management	International management refers to the management of business operations conducted in more than one country.
Accretion	In finance, accretion is the change in the price of a bond bought at a discount between the original price and the par value of the bond.
Integration	Economic integration refers to reducing barriers among countries to transactions and to movements of goods, capital, and labor, including harmonization of laws, regulations, and standards. Integrated markets theoretically function as a unified market.
World Bank	The World Bank is a group of five international organizations responsible for providing finance and advice to countries for the purposes of economic development and poverty reduction, and for encouraging and safeguarding international investment.
Labor	People's physical and mental talents and efforts that are used to help produce goods and services are called labor.
Fund	Independent accounting entity with a self-balancing set of accounts segregated for the purposes of carrying on specific activities is referred to as a fund.
International Monetary Fund	The International Monetary Fund is the international organization entrusted with overseeing the global financial system by monitoring exchange rates and balance of payments, as well as offering technical and financial assistance when asked.
World Health Organization	The World Health Organization is a specialized agency of the United Nations, acting as a coordinating authority on international public health, headquartered in Geneva, Switzerland. It's constitution

Chapter 1. INTRODUCTION

Chapter 1. INTRODUCTION

	states that its mission "is the attainment by all peoples of the highest possible level of health". Its major task is to combat disease, especially key infectious diseases, and to promote the general health of the peoples of the world.
World Trade Organization	The World Trade Organization is an international, multilateral organization, which sets the rules for the global trading system and resolves disputes between its member states, all of whom are signatories to its approximately 30 agreements.
Union	A worker association that bargains with employers over wages and working conditions is called a union.
International Atomic Energy Agency	International Atomic Energy Agency was established as an autonomous organization on July 29, 1957. It seeks to promote the peaceful use of nuclear energy and to inhibit its use for military purposes. United States President Dwight D. Eisenhower envisioned, in his "Atoms for Peace" speech before the UN General Assembly in 1953, the creation of this international body to control and develop the use of atomic energy.
Globalization	The increasing world-wide integration of markets for goods, services and capital that attracted special attention in the late 1990s is called globalization.
Fragmentation	Fragmentation refers to the splitting of production processes into separate parts that can be done in different locations, including in different countries.
Technological change	The introduction of new methods of production or new products intended to increase the productivity of existing inputs or to raise marginal products is a technological change.
Continuity	A media scheduling strategy where a continuous pattern of advertising is used over the time span of the advertising campaign is continuity.
Domestic	From or in one's own country. A domestic producer is one that produces inside the home country. A domestic price is the price inside the home country. Opposite of 'foreign' or 'world.'.
Manufactured good	A manufactured good refers to goods that have been processed in any way.
Stock market	An organized marketplace in which common stocks are traded. In the United States, the largest stock market is the New York Stock Exchange, on which are traded the stocks of the largest U.S. companies.
Market	A market is, as defined in economics, a social arrangement that allows buyers and sellers to discover information and carry out a voluntary exchange of goods or services.
Stock	In financial terminology, stock is the capital raized by a corporation, through the issuance and sale of shares.
Financial institution	A financial institution acts as an agent that provides financial services for its clients. Financial institutions generally fall under financial regulation from a government authority.
Localization	As an element of wireless marketing strategy, transmitting messages that are relevant to the user's current geographical location are referred to as localization.
Production	The creation of finished goods and services using the factors of production: land, labor, capital, entrepreneurship, and knowledge.
Globalization of production	Globalization of production refers to trends by individual firms to disperse parts of their productive processes to different locations around the globe to take advantage of differences in cost and quality of factors of production.
Police power	The states' power to regulate to promote the public health, safety, morals, and welfare is police power.
Multilateralism	Multilateralism is an international relations term that refers to multiple countries working in concert.

Chapter 1. INTRODUCTION

Chapter 1. INTRODUCTION

Journal	Book of original entry, in which transactions are recorded in a general ledger system, is referred to as a journal.
Collaboration	Collaboration occurs when the interaction between groups is very important to goal attainment and the goals are compatible. Wherein people work together —applying both to the work of individuals as well as larger collectives and societies.
Property	Assets defined in the broadest legal sense. Property includes the unrealized receivables of a cash basis taxpayer, but not services rendered.
Reciprocity	An industrial buying practice in which two organizations agree to purchase each other's products and services is called reciprocity.
Gain	In finance, gain is a profit or an increase in value of an investment such as a stock or bond. Gain is calculated by fair market value or the proceeds from the sale of the investment minus the sum of the purchase price and all costs associated with it.
Corporation	A legal entity chartered by a state or the Federal government that is distinct and separate from the individuals who own it is a corporation. This separation gives the corporation unique powers which other legal entities lack.
Multinational corporations	Firms that own production facilities in two or more countries and produce and sell their products globally are referred to as multinational corporations.
Multinational corporation	An organization that manufactures and markets products in many different countries and has multinational stock ownership and multinational management is referred to as multinational corporation.
Primary factor	Primary factor refers to an input that exists as a stock, providing services that contribute to production. The stock is not used up in production, although it may deteriorate with use, providing a smaller flow of services later.
Variable	A variable is something measured by a number; it is used to analyze what happens to other things when the size of that number changes.
Status quo	Status quo is a Latin term meaning the present, current, existing state of affairs.
Neoliberalism	A view of the world that favors social justice while also emphasizing economic growth, efficiency, and the benefits of free markets is called neoliberalism.
Configuration	An organization's shape, which reflects the division of labor and the means of coordinating the divided tasks is configuration.
Contract	A contract is a "promise" or an "agreement" that is enforced or recognized by the law. In the civil law, a contract is considered to be part of the general law of obligations.
Argument	The discussion by counsel for the respective parties of their contentions on the law and the facts of the case being tried in order to aid the jury in arriving at a correct and just conclusion is called argument.
Political economy	Early name for the discipline of economics. A field within economics encompassing several alternatives to neoclassical economics, including Marxist economics. Also called radical political economy.
Option	A contract that gives the purchaser the option to buy or sell the underlying financial instrument at a specified price, called the exercise price or strike price, within a specific period of time.
Negotiation	Negotiation is the process whereby interested parties resolve disputes, agree upon courses of action, bargain for individual or collective advantage, and/or attempt to craft outcomes which serve their mutual interests.
Framing	Framing refers to the tendency for a decision maker to be swayed by whether a decision is pitched as a positive or negative.

Chapter 1. INTRODUCTION

Chapter 1. INTRODUCTION

Aid	Assistance provided by countries and by international institutions such as the World Bank to developing countries in the form of monetary grants, loans at low interest rates, in kind, or a combination of these is called aid. Aid can also refer to assistance of any type rendered to benefit some group or individual.
Trade in services	Trade in services refers to the provision of a service to buyers within or from one country by a firm in or from another country.
International policy coordination	International policy coordination refers to agreements among countries to enact policies cooperatively.
Openness	Openness refers to the extent to which an economy is open, often measured by the ratio of its trade to
Distribution	Distribution in economics, the manner in which total output and income is distributed among individuals or factors.
Credit	Credit refers to a recording as positive in the balance of payments, any transaction that gives rise to a payment into the country, such as an export, the sale of an asset, or borrowing from abroad.
Credit worthiness	Credit worthiness is the risk of loss due to a counterparty defaulting on a contract, or more generally the risk of loss due to some "credit event".
Hierarchy	A system of grouping people in an organization according to rank from the top down in which all subordinate managers must report to one person is called a hierarchy.
Discount	The difference between the face value of a bond and its selling price, when a bond is sold for less than its face value it's referred to as a discount.
Elasticity	In economics, elasticity is the ratio of the incremental percentage change in one variable with respect to an incremental percentage change in another variable. Elasticity is usually expressed as a positive number (i.e., an absolute value) when the sign is already clear from context.

Go to **Cram101.com** for the Practice Tests for this Chapter.

Chapter 1. INTRODUCTION

Chapter 2. A GREAT EXPERIMENT: THE LEAGUE OF NATIONS

Sovereignty	A country or region's power and ability to rule itself and manage its own affairs. Some feel that membership in international organizations such as the WTO is a threat to their sovereignty.
Policy	Similar to a script in that a policy can be a less than completely rational decision-making method. Involves the use of a pre-existing set of decision steps for any problem that presents itself.
United Nations	An international organization created by multilateral treaty in 1945 to promote social and economic cooperation among nations and to protect human rights is the United Nations.
Interest	In finance and economics, interest is the price paid by a borrower for the use of a lender's money. In other words, interest is the amount of paid to "rent" money for a period of time.
Points	Loan origination fees that may be deductible as interest by a buyer of property. A seller of property who pays points reduces the selling price by the amount of the points paid for the buyer.
Committee	A long-lasting, sometimes permanent team in the organization structure created to deal with tasks that recur regularly is the committee.
Draft	A signed, written order by which one party instructs another party to pay a specified sum to a third party, at sight or at a specific date is a draft.
Capital	Capital generally refers to financial wealth, especially that used to start or maintain a business. In classical economics, capital is one of four factors of production, the others being land and labor and entrepreneurship.
Delegation	Delegation is the handing of a task over to another person, usually a subordinate. It is the assignment of authority and responsibility to another person to carry out specific activities.
Treaties	The first source of international law, consisting of agreements or contracts between two or more nations that are formally signed by an authorized representative and ratified by the supreme power of each nation are called treaties.
Covenant	A covenant is a signed written agreement between two or more parties. Also referred to as a contract.
Objection	In the trial of a case the formal remonstrance made by counsel to something that has been said or done, in order to obtain the court's ruling thereon is an objection.
Incorporation	Incorporation is the forming of a new corporation. The corporation may be a business, a non-profit organization or even a government of a new city or town.
Recruitment	Recruitment refers to the set of activities used to obtain a sufficient number of the right people at the right time; its purpose is to select those who best meet the needs of the organization.
Authority	Authority in agency law, refers to an agent's ability to affect his principal's legal relations with third parties. Also used to refer to an actor's legal power or ability to do something. In addition, sometimes used to refer to a statute, case, or other legal source that justifies a particular result.
Argument	The discussion by counsel for the respective parties of their contentions on the law and the facts of the case being tried in order to aid the jury in arriving at a correct and just conclusion is called argument.
Union	A worker association that bargains with employers over wages and working conditions is called a union.

Go to **Cram101.com** for the Practice Tests for this Chapter.

Chapter 2. A GREAT EXPERIMENT: THE LEAGUE OF NATIONS

Chapter 2. A GREAT EXPERIMENT: THE LEAGUE OF NATIONS

Consideration	Consideration in contract law, a basic requirement for an enforceable agreement under traditional contract principles, defined in this text as legal value, bargained for and given in exchange for an act or promise. In corporation law, cash or property contributed to a corporation in exchange for shares, or a promise to contribute such cash or property.
Negotiation	Negotiation is the process whereby interested parties resolve disputes, agree upon courses of action, bargain for individual or collective advantage, and/or attempt to craft outcomes which serve their mutual interests.
Arbitration	Arbitration is a form of mediation or conciliation, where the mediating party is given power by the disputant parties to settle the dispute by making a finding. In practice arbitration is generally used as a substitute for judicial systems, particularly when the judicial processes are viewed as too slow, expensive or biased. Arbitration is also used by communities which lack formal law, as a substitute for formal law.
Indirect cost	Indirect cost refers to a cost that cannot be traced to a particular department.
Contribution	In business organization law, the cash or property contributed to a business by its owners is referred to as contribution.
Industry	A group of firms that produce identical or similar products is an industry. It is also used specifically to refer to an area of economic production focused on manufacturing which involves large amounts of capital investment before any profit can be realized, also called "heavy industry".
Labor	People's physical and mental talents and efforts that are used to help produce goods and services are called labor.
International trade	The export of goods and services from a country and the import of goods and services into a country is referred to as the international trade.
Promotion	Promotion refers to all the techniques sellers use to motivate people to buy products or services. An attempt by marketers to inform people about products and to persuade them to participate in an exchange.
Trust	An arrangement in which shareholders of independent firms agree to give up their stock in exchange for trust certificates that entitle them to a share of the trust's common profits.
Annual report	An annual report is prepared by corporate management that presents financial information including financial statements, footnotes, and the management discussion and analysis.
Compliance	A type of influence process where a receiver accepts the position advocated by a source to obtain favorable outcomes or to avoid punishment is the compliance.
Tangible	Having a physical existence is referred to as the tangible. Personal property other than real estate, such as cars, boats, stocks, or other assets.
Balance	In banking and accountancy, the outstanding balance is the amount of money owned, (or due), that remains in a deposit account (or a loan account) at a given date, after all past remittances, payments and withdrawal have been accounted for. It can be positive (then, in the balance sheet of a firm, it is an asset) or negative (a liability).
Brief	Brief refers to a statement of a party's case or legal arguments, usually prepared by an attorney. Also used to make legal arguments before appellate courts.
Precedent	A previously decided court decision that is recognized as authority for the disposition of future decisions is a precedent.
Operation	A standardized method or technique that is performed repetitively, often on different materials resulting in different finished goods is called an operation.

Go to Cram101.com for the Practice Tests for this Chapter.

Chapter 2. A GREAT EXPERIMENT: THE LEAGUE OF NATIONS

Chapter 2. A GREAT EXPERIMENT: THE LEAGUE OF NATIONS

Credit	Credit refers to a recording as positive in the balance of payments, any transaction that gives rise to a payment into the country, such as an export, the sale of an asset, or borrowing from abroad.
Administration	Administration refers to the management and direction of the affairs of governments and institutions; a collective term for all policymaking officials of a government; the execution and implementation of public policy.
Leadership	Management merely consists of leadership applied to business situations; or in other words: management forms a sub-set of the broader process of leadership.
Service	Service refers to a "non tangible product" that is not embodied in a physical good and that typically effects some change in another product, person, or institution. Contrasts with good.
Private law	Private law is that part of a legal system which is part of the jus commune that involves relationships between individuals, such as the law of contracts or torts, as it is called in the common law, and the law of obligations as it is called in civilian legal systems.
Principal	In agency law, one under whose direction an agent acts and for whose benefit that agent acts is a principal.
Budget	Budget refers to an account, usually for a year, of the planned expenditures and the expected receipts of an entity. For a government, the receipts are tax revenues.
Economy	The income, expenditures, and resources that affect the cost of running a business and household are called an economy.
Expense	In accounting, an expense represents an event in which an asset is used up or a liability is incurred. In terms of the accounting equation, expenses reduce owners' equity.
Utility	Utility refers to the want-satisfying power of a good or service; the satisfaction or pleasure a consumer obtains from the consumption of a good or service.
Property	Assets defined in the broadest legal sense. Property includes the unrealized receivables of a cash basis taxpayer, but not services rendered.
Pact	Pact refers to a set of principles endorsed by 21 of the largest U.S. ad agencies aimed at improving the research used in preparing and testing ads, providing a better creative product for clients, and controlling the cost of TV commercials.
Supply	Supply is the aggregate amount of any material good that can be called into being at a certain price point; it comprises one half of the equation of supply and demand. In classical economic theory, a curve representing supply is one of the factors that produce price.
Complaint	The pleading in a civil case in which the plaintiff states his claim and requests relief is called complaint. In the common law, it is a formal legal document that sets out the basic facts and legal reasons that the filing party (the plaintiffs) believes are sufficient to support a claim against another person, persons, entity or entities (the defendants) that entitles the plaintiff(s) to a remedy (either money damages or injunctive relief).
Concession	A concession is a business operated under a contract or license associated with a degree of exclusivity in exploiting a business within a certain geographical area. For example, sports arenas or public parks may have concession stands; and public services such as water supply may be operated as concessions.
Regulation	Regulation refers to restrictions state and federal laws place on business with regard to the conduct of its activities.
Economic sanction	A economic sanction can vary from imposing import duties on goods from, or blocking the export of certain goods to the target country, to a full naval blockade of its ports in an

Chapter 2. A GREAT EXPERIMENT: THE LEAGUE OF NATIONS

Chapter 2. A GREAT EXPERIMENT: THE LEAGUE OF NATIONS

	effort to verify, and curb or block specified imported goods.
Cooperative	A business owned and controlled by the people who use it, producers, consumers, or workers with similar needs who pool their resources for mutual gain is called cooperative.
Embargo	Embargo refers to the prohibition of some category of trade. May apply to exports and/or imports, of particular products or of all trade, vis a vis the world or a particular country or countries.
Conciliation	A form of mediation in which the parties choose an interested third party to act as the mediator is referred to as conciliation.
Security	Security refers to a claim on the borrower future income that is sold by the borrower to the lender. A security is a type of transferable interest representing financial value.
Internationa-ization	Internationalization refers to another term for fragmentation. Used by Grossman and Helpman.
Plea	A plea is an answer to a declaration or complaint or any material allegation of fact therein that, if untrue, would defeat the action. In criminal procedure, a plea is the matter that the accused, on his arraignment, alleges in answer to the charge against him.
Gap	In December of 1995, Gap became the first major North American retailer to accept independent monitoring of the working conditions in a contract factory producing its garments. Gap is the largest specialty retailer in the United States.
Compromise	Compromise occurs when the interaction is moderately important to meeting goals and the goals are neither completely compatible nor completely incompatible.
Agent	A person who makes economic decisions for another economic actor. A hired manager operates as an agent for a firm's owner.
Instrument	Instrument refers to an economic variable that is controlled by policy makers and can be used to influence other variables, called targets. Examples are monetary and fiscal policies used to achieve external and internal balance.
Fund	Independent accounting entity with a self-balancing set of accounts segregated for the purposes of carrying on specific activities is referred to as a fund.
Reorganization	Reorganization occurs, among other instances, when one corporation acquires another in a merger or acquisition, a single corporation divides into two or more entities, or a corporation makes a substantial change in its capital structure.
Composition	An out-of-court settlement in which creditors agree to accept a fractional settlement on their original claim is referred to as composition.
Assessment	Collecting information and providing feedback to employees about their behavior, communication style, or skills is an assessment.
Trend	Trend refers to the long-term movement of an economic variable, such as its average rate of increase or decrease over enough years to encompass several business cycles.
Administrative agency	Administrative agency refers to a unit of government charged with the administration of particular laws. In the United States, those most important for administering laws related to international trade are the ITC and ITA.
Innovation	Innovation refers to the first commercially successful introduction of a new product, the use of a new method of production, or the creation of a new form of business organization.
Comprehensive	A comprehensive refers to a layout accurate in size, color, scheme, and other necessary details to show how a final ad will look. For presentation only, never for reproduction.

Go to **Cram101.com** for the Practice Tests for this Chapter.

Chapter 2. A GREAT EXPERIMENT: THE LEAGUE OF NATIONS

Chapter 2. A GREAT EXPERIMENT: THE LEAGUE OF NATIONS

Status quo | Status quo is a Latin term meaning the present, current, existing state of affairs.

Channel | Channel, in communications (sometimes called communications channel), refers to the medium used to convey information from a sender (or transmitter) to a receiver.

Domestic | From or in one's own country. A domestic producer is one that produces inside the home country. A domestic price is the price inside the home country. Opposite of 'foreign' or 'world.'.

Prejudice | Prejudice is, as the name implies, the process of "pre-judging" something. It implies coming to a judgment on a subject before learning where the preponderance of evidence actually lies, or forming a judgment without direct experience.

Chapter 2. A GREAT EXPERIMENT: THE LEAGUE OF NATIONS

Chapter 3. THE GENESIS OF THE UNITED NATIONS

Interest	In finance and economics, interest is the price paid by a borrower for the use of a lender's money. In other words, interest is the amount of paid to "rent" money for a period of time.
United Nations	An international organization created by multilateral treaty in 1945 to promote social and economic cooperation among nations and to protect human rights is the United Nations.
Balance	In banking and accountancy, the outstanding balance is the amount of money owned, (or due), that remains in a deposit account (or a loan account) at a given date, after all past remittances, payments and withdrawal have been accounted for. It can be positive (then, in the balance sheet of a firm, it is an asset) or negative (a liability).
Covenant	A covenant is a signed written agreement between two or more parties. Also referred to as a contract.
Charter	Charter refers to an instrument or authority from the sovereign power bestowing the right or power to do business under the corporate form of organization. Also, the organic law of a city or town, and representing a portion of the statute law of the state.
Foundation	A Foundation is a type of philanthropic organization set up by either individuals or institutions as a legal entity (either as a corporation or trust) with the purpose of distributing grants to support causes in line with the goals of the foundation.
Committee	A long-lasting, sometimes permanent team in the organization structure created to deal with tasks that recur regularly is the committee.
Management	Management characterizes the process of leading and directing all or part of an organization, often a business, through the deployment and manipulation of resources. Early twentieth-century management writer Mary Parker Follett defined management as "the art of getting things done through people."
Commerce	Commerce is the exchange of something of value between two entities. It is the central mechanism from which capitalism is derived.
Labor	People's physical and mental talents and efforts that are used to help produce goods and services are called labor.
American Federation of Labor	American Federation of Labor refers to an organization of craft unions that championed fundamental labor issues; founded in 1886.
Comprehensive	A comprehensive refers to a layout accurate in size, color, scheme, and other necessary details to show how a final ad will look. For presentation only, never for reproduction.
Public interest	The universal label that political actors wrap around the policies and programs that they advocate is referred to as public interest.
Leadership	Management merely consists of leadership applied to business situations; or in other words: management forms a sub-set of the broader process of leadership.
Authority	Authority in agency law, refers to an agent's ability to affect his principal's legal relations with third parties. Also used to refer to an actor's legal power or ability to do something. In addition, sometimes used to refer to a statute, case, or other legal source that justifies a particular result.
Union	A worker association that bargains with employers over wages and working conditions is called a union.
Scope	Scope of a project is the sum total of all projects products and their requirements or features.
Endowment	Endowment refers to the amount of something that a person or country simply has, rather than

Chapter 3. THE GENESIS OF THE UNITED NATIONS

Chapter 3. THE GENESIS OF THE UNITED NATIONS

	their having somehow to acquire it.
Cooperative	A business owned and controlled by the people who use it, producers, consumers, or workers with similar needs who pool their resources for mutual gain is called cooperative.
Enterprise	Enterprise refers to another name for a business organization. Other similar terms are business firm, sometimes simply business, sometimes simply firm, as well as company, and entity.
International law	Law that governs affairs between nations and that regulates transactions between individuals and businesses of different countries is an international law.
Conciliation	A form of mediation in which the parties choose an interested third party to act as the mediator is referred to as conciliation.
Policy	Similar to a script in that a policy can be a less than completely rational decision-making method. Involves the use of a pre-existing set of decision steps for any problem that presents itself.
Private sector	The households and business firms of the economy are referred to as private sector.
Personnel	A collective term for all of the employees of an organization. Personnel is also commonly used to refer to the personnel management function or the organizational unit responsible for administering personnel programs.
Security	Security refers to a claim on the borrower future income that is sold by the borrower to the lender. A security is a type of transferable interest representing financial value.
Decentralization	Decentralization is the process of redistributing decision-making closer to the point of service or action. This gives freedom to managers at lower levels of the organization to make decisions.
Bretton Woods	A 1944 conference in which representatives of 40 countries met to design a new international monetary system is referred to as the Bretton Woods conference.
Fund	Independent accounting entity with a self-balancing set of accounts segregated for the purposes of carrying on specific activities is referred to as a fund.
International Monetary Fund	The International Monetary Fund is the international organization entrusted with overseeing the global financial system by monitoring exchange rates and balance of payments, as well as offering technical and financial assistance when asked.
Bretton Woods conference	The United Nations Monetary and Financial Conference, commonly known as Bretton Woods conference, was a gathering of 730 delegates from all 45 Allied nations at the Mount Washington Hotel. The conference was held from 1 July to 22 July 1944, when the Agreements were signed to set up the International Bank for Reconstruction and Development, GATT and the International Monetary Fund, to regulate the international monetary and financial order after World War II.
Preference	The act of a debtor in paying or securing one or more of his creditors in a manner more favorable to them than to other creditors or to the exclusion of such other creditors is a preference. In the absence of statute, a preference is perfectly good, but to be legal it must be bona fide, and not a mere subterfuge of the debtor to secure a future benefit to himself or to prevent the application of his property to his debts.
Accommodation	Accommodation is a term used to describe a delivery of nonconforming goods meant as a partial performance of a contract for the sale of goods, where a full performance is not possible.
Functional organization	Functional organization is a method of organization in which chapters and sections of a manual correspond to business functions, not specific departments or work groups.

Go to Cram101.com for the Practice Tests for this Chapter.

Chapter 3. THE GENESIS OF THE UNITED NATIONS

Chapter 3. THE GENESIS OF THE UNITED NATIONS

Social Security	Social security primarily refers to a field of social welfare concerned with social protection, or protection against socially recognized conditions, including poverty, old age, disability, unemployment, families with children and others.
Prime minister	The Prime Minister of the United Kingdom of Great Britain and Northern Ireland is the head of government and so exercises many of the executive functions nominally vested in the Sovereign, who is head of state. According to custom, the Prime Minister and the Cabinet (which he or she heads) are accountable for their actions to Parliament, of which they are members by (modern) convention.
Compromise	Compromise occurs when the interaction is moderately important to meeting goals and the goals are neither completely compatible nor completely incompatible.
Points	Loan origination fees that may be deductible as interest by a buyer of property. A seller of property who pays points reduces the selling price by the amount of the points paid for the buyer.
Pledge	In law a pledge (also pawn) is a bailment of personal property as a security for some debt or engagement.
Goodwill	Goodwill is an important accounting concept that describes the value of a business entity not directly attributable to its tangible assets and liabilities.
Draft	A signed, written order by which one party instructs another party to pay a specified sum to a third party, at sight or at a specific date is a draft.
Exchange	The trade of things of value between buyer and seller so that each is better off after the trade is called the exchange.
Estate	An estate is the totality of the legal rights, interests, entitlements and obligations attaching to property. In the context of wills and probate, it refers to the totality of the property which the deceased owned or in which some interest was held.
Big Four	The Big Four is a group of international accountancy and professional services firms that handles the vast majority of audits for publicly traded companies as well as many private companies. The members of the group are PricewaterhouseCoopers, Deloitte Touche Tohmatsu, Ernst & Young and KPMG.
Incorporation	Incorporation is the forming of a new corporation. The corporation may be a business, a non-profit organization or even a government of a new city or town.
Subsidiary	A company that is controlled by another company or corporation is a subsidiary.
Gap	In December of 1995, Gap became the first major North American retailer to accept independent monitoring of the working conditions in a contract factory producing its garments. Gap is the largest specialty retailer in the United States.
Privilege	Generally, a legal right to engage in conduct that would otherwise result in legal liability is a privilege. Privileges are commonly classified as absolute or conditional. Occasionally, privilege is also used to denote a legal right to refrain from particular behavior.
Concession	A concession is a business operated under a contract or license associated with a degree of exclusivity in exploiting a business within a certain geographical area. For example, sports arenas or public parks may have concession stands; and public services such as water supply may be operated as concessions.
Trust	An arrangement in which shareholders of independent firms agree to give up their stock in exchange for trust certificates that entitle them to a share of the trust's common profits.
Delegation	Delegation is the handing of a task over to another person, usually a subordinate. It is the assignment of authority and responsibility to another person to carry out specific

Chapter 3. THE GENESIS OF THE UNITED NATIONS

Chapter 3. THE GENESIS OF THE UNITED NATIONS

	activities.
Jurisdiction	The power of a court to hear and decide a case is called jurisdiction. It is the practical authority granted to a formally constituted body or to a person to deal with and make pronouncements on legal matters and, by implication, to administer justice within a defined area of responsibility.
Host country	The country in which the parent-country organization seeks to locate or has already located a facility is a host country.
Service	Service refers to a "non tangible product" that is not embodied in a physical good and that typically effects some change in another product, person, or institution. Contrasts with good.
Objection	In the trial of a case the formal remonstrance made by counsel to something that has been said or done, in order to obtain the court's ruling thereon is an objection.
Gain	In finance, gain is a profit or an increase in value of an investment such as a stock or bond. Gain is calculated by fair market value or the proceeds from the sale of the investment minus the sum of the purchase price and all costs associated with it.
Appeal	Appeal refers to the act of asking an appellate court to overturn a decision after the trial court's final judgment has been entered.
Administration	Administration refers to the management and direction of the affairs of governments and institutions; a collective term for all policymaking officials of a government; the execution and implementation of public policy.
Welfare	Welfare refers to the economic well being of an individual, group, or economy. For individuals, it is conceptualized by a utility function. For groups, including countries and the world, it is a tricky philosophical concept, since individuals fare differently.
Statute	A statute is a formal, written law of a country or state, written and enacted by its legislative authority, perhaps to then be ratified by the highest executive in the government, and finally published.
Instrument	Instrument refers to an economic variable that is controlled by policy makers and can be used to influence other variables, called targets. Examples are monetary and fiscal policies used to achieve external and internal balance.
Principal	In agency law, one under whose direction an agent acts and for whose benefit that agent acts is a principal.

Chapter 3. THE GENESIS OF THE UNITED NATIONS

Chapter 4. BASIC PRINCIPLES AND ORGANIZATION OF THE UNITED NATIONS

Charter	Charter refers to an instrument or authority from the sovereign power bestowing the right or power to do business under the corporate form of organization. Also, the organic law of a city or town, and representing a portion of the statute law of the state.
International law	Law that governs affairs between nations and that regulates transactions between individuals and businesses of different countries is an international law.
Organizational structure	Organizational structure is the way in which the interrelated groups of an organization are constructed. From a managerial point of view the main concerns are ensuring effective communication and coordination.
United Nations	An international organization created by multilateral treaty in 1945 to promote social and economic cooperation among nations and to protect human rights is the United Nations.
Welfare	Welfare refers to the economic well being of an individual, group, or economy. For individuals, it is conceptualized by a utility function. For groups, including countries and the world, it is a tricky philosophical concept, since individuals fare differently.
Points	Loan origination fees that may be deductible as interest by a buyer of property. A seller of property who pays points reduces the selling price by the amount of the points paid for the buyer.
Security	Security refers to a claim on the borrower future income that is sold by the borrower to the lender. A security is a type of transferable interest representing financial value.
Instrument	Instrument refers to an economic variable that is controlled by policy makers and can be used to influence other variables, called targets. Examples are monetary and fiscal policies used to achieve external and internal balance.
Shares	Shares refer to an equity security, representing a shareholder's ownership of a corporation. Shares are one of a finite number of equal portions in the capital of a company, entitling the owner to a proportion of distributed, non-reinvested profits known as dividends and to a portion of the value of the company in case of liquidation.
Subsidiary	A company that is controlled by another company or corporation is a subsidiary.
Draft	A signed, written order by which one party instructs another party to pay a specified sum to a third party, at sight or at a specific date is a draft.
Interest	In finance and economics, interest is the price paid by a borrower for the use of a lender's money. In other words, interest is the amount of paid to "rent" money for a period of time.
Operation	A standardized method or technique that is performed repetitively, often on different materials resulting in different finished goods is called an operation.
Assessment	Collecting information and providing feedback to employees about their behavior, communication style, or skills is an assessment.
Assignment	A transfer of property or some right or interest is referred to as assignment.
Sovereignty	A country or region's power and ability to rule itself and manage its own affairs. Some feel that membership in international organizations such as the WTO is a threat to their sovereignty.
Authority	Authority in agency law, refers to an agent's ability to affect his principal's legal relations with third parties. Also used to refer to an actor's legal power or ability to do something. In addition, sometimes used to refer to a statute, case, or other legal source that justifies a particular result.
Attest	To bear witness to is called attest. To affirm, certify by oath or signature. It is an official act establishing authenticity.

Chapter 4. BASIC PRINCIPLES AND ORGANIZATION OF THE UNITED NATIONS

Collective responsibility	Cabinet collective responsibility is constitutional convention in the states that use the Westminster System. It means that members of the Cabinet must publicly support all governmental decisions made in Cabinet, even if they do not privately agree with them.
Impossibility	A doctrine under which a party to a contract is relieved of his or her duty to perform when that performance has become impossible because of the occurrence of an event unforeseen at the time of contracting is referred to as impossibility.
Domestic	From or in one's own country. A domestic producer is one that produces inside the home country. A domestic price is the price inside the home country. Opposite of 'foreign' or 'world.'.
Jurisdiction	The power of a court to hear and decide a case is called jurisdiction. It is the practical authority granted to a formally constituted body or to a person to deal with and make pronouncements on legal matters and, by implication, to administer justice within a defined area of responsibility.
Channel	Channel, in communications (sometimes called communications channel), refers to the medium used to convey information from a sender (or transmitter) to a receiver.
Cooperative	A business owned and controlled by the people who use it, producers, consumers, or workers with similar needs who pool their resources for mutual gain is called cooperative.
Covenant	A covenant is a signed written agreement between two or more parties. Also referred to as a contract.
Privilege	Generally, a legal right to engage in conduct that would otherwise result in legal liability is a privilege. Privileges are commonly classified as absolute or conditional. Occasionally, privilege is also used to denote a legal right to refrain from particular behavior.
Immunity	Granted by law, immunity is the assurance that someone will be exempt from prosecution.
Agent	A person who makes economic decisions for another economic actor. A hired manager operates as an agent for a firm's owner.
Principal	In agency law, one under whose direction an agent acts and for whose benefit that agent acts is a principal.
Scope	Scope of a project is the sum total of all projects products and their requirements or features.
Investment	Investment refers to spending for the production and accumulation of capital and additions to inventories. In a financial sense, buying an asset with the expectation of making a return.
Standing	Standing refers to the legal requirement that anyone seeking to challenge a particular action in court must demonstrate that such action substantially affects his legitimate interests before he will be entitled to bring suit.
Corporation	A legal entity chartered by a state or the Federal government that is distinct and separate from the individuals who own it is a corporation. This separation gives the corporation unique powers which other legal entities lack.
World Bank	The World Bank is a group of five international organizations responsible for providing finance and advice to countries for the purposes of economic development and poverty reduction, and for encouraging and safeguarding international investment.
Committee	A long-lasting, sometimes permanent team in the organization structure created to deal with tasks that recur regularly is the committee.
Property	Assets defined in the broadest legal sense. Property includes the unrealized receivables of a cash basis taxpayer, but not services rendered.

Chapter 4. BASIC PRINCIPLES AND ORGANIZATION OF THE UNITED NATIONS

Chapter 4. BASIC PRINCIPLES AND ORGANIZATION OF THE UNITED NATIONS

Ad hoc	Ad hoc is a Latin phrase which means "for this purpose." It generally signifies a solution that has been tailored to a specific purpose and is makeshift and non-general, such as a handcrafted network protocol or a specific-purpose equation, as opposed to general solutions.
Union	A worker association that bargains with employers over wages and working conditions is called a union.
Fund	Independent accounting entity with a self-balancing set of accounts segregated for the purposes of carrying on specific activities is referred to as a fund.
World Trade Organization	The World Trade Organization is an international, multilateral organization, which sets the rules for the global trading system and resolves disputes between its member states, all of whom are signatories to its approximately 30 agreements.
Intellectual property	In law, intellectual property is an umbrella term for various legal entitlements which attach to certain types of information, ideas, or other intangibles in their expressed form. The holder of this legal entitlement is generally entitled to exercise various exclusive rights in relation to its subject matter.
Raw material	Raw material refers to a good that has not been transformed by production; a primary product.
Delegation	Delegation is the handing of a task over to another person, usually a subordinate. It is the assignment of authority and responsibility to another person to carry out specific activities.
Allocate	Allocate refers to the assignment of income for various tax purposes. A multistate corporation's nonbusiness income usually is distributed to the state where the nonbusiness assets are located; it is not apportioned with the rest of the entity's income.
Comprehensive	A comprehensive refers to a layout accurate in size, color, scheme, and other necessary details to show how a final ad will look. For presentation only, never for reproduction.
Grant	Grant refers to an intergovernmental transfer of funds. Since the New Deal, state and local governments have become increasingly dependent upon federal grants for an almost infinite variety of programs.
Policy	Similar to a script in that a policy can be a less than completely rational decision-making method. Involves the use of a pre-existing set of decision steps for any problem that presents itself.
Applicant	In many tribunal and administrative law suits, the person who initiates the claim is called the applicant.
Aid	Assistance provided by countries and by international institutions such as the World Bank to developing countries in the form of monetary grants, loans at low interest rates, in kind, or a combination of these is called aid. Aid can also refer to assistance of any type rendered to benefit some group or individual.
Collaboration	Collaboration occurs when the interaction between groups is very important to goal attainment and the goals are compatible. Wherein people work together —applying both to the work of individuals as well as larger collectives and societies.
Adoption	In corporation law, a corporation's acceptance of a pre-incorporation contract by action of its board of directors, by which the corporation becomes liable on the contract, is referred to as adoption.
Service	Service refers to a "non tangible product" that is not embodied in a physical good and that typically effects some change in another product, person, or institution. Contrasts with good.
Consideration	Consideration in contract law, a basic requirement for an enforceable agreement under

Chapter 4. BASIC PRINCIPLES AND ORGANIZATION OF THE UNITED NATIONS

Chapter 4. BASIC PRINCIPLES AND ORGANIZATION OF THE UNITED NATIONS

	traditional contract principles, defined in this text as legal value, bargained for and given in exchange for an act or promise. In corporation law, cash or property contributed to a corporation in exchange for shares, or a promise to contribute such cash or property.
Frequency	Frequency refers to the speed of the up and down movements of a fluctuating economic variable; that is, the number of times per unit of time that the variable completes a cycle of up and down movement.
Firm	An organization that employs resources to produce a good or service for profit and owns and operates one or more plants is referred to as a firm.
Regulation	Regulation refers to restrictions state and federal laws place on business with regard to the conduct of its activities.
Trust	An arrangement in which shareholders of independent firms agree to give up their stock in exchange for trust certificates that entitle them to a share of the trust's common profits.
Trustee	An independent party appointed to represent the bondholders is referred to as a trustee.
Gap	In December of 1995, Gap became the first major North American retailer to accept independent monitoring of the working conditions in a contract factory producing its garments. Gap is the largest specialty retailer in the United States.
Accommodation	Accommodation is a term used to describe a delivery of nonconforming goods meant as a partial performance of a contract for the sale of goods, where a full performance is not possible.
Utility	Utility refers to the want-satisfying power of a good or service; the satisfaction or pleasure a consumer obtains from the consumption of a good or service.
Supply	Supply is the aggregate amount of any material good that can be called into being at a certain price point; it comprises one half of the equation of supply and demand. In classical economic theory, a curve representing supply is one of the factors that produce price.
Labor	People's physical and mental talents and efforts that are used to help produce goods and services are called labor.
Standardization	Standardization, in the context related to technologies and industries, is the process of establishing a technical standard among competing entities in a market, where this will bring benefits without hurting competition.
Preparation	Preparation refers to usually the first stage in the creative process. It includes education and formal training.
Personnel	A collective term for all of the employees of an organization. Personnel is also commonly used to refer to the personnel management function or the organizational unit responsible for administering personnel programs.
Demographic	A demographic is a term used in marketing and broadcasting, to describe a demographic grouping or a market segment.
Conflict of interest	A conflict that occurs when a corporate officer or director enters into a transaction with the corporation in which he or she has a personal interest is a conflict of interest.
Structural change	Changes in the relative importance of different areas of an economy over time, usually measured in terms of their share of output, employment, or total spending is structural change.
Administration	Administration refers to the management and direction of the affairs of governments and institutions; a collective term for all policymaking officials of a government; the execution and implementation of public policy.
Compliance	A type of influence process where a receiver accepts the position advocated by a source to

Chapter 4. BASIC PRINCIPLES AND ORGANIZATION OF THE UNITED NATIONS

	obtain favorable outcomes or to avoid punishment is the compliance.
Publicity	Publicity refers to any information about an individual, product, or organization that's distributed to the public through the media and that's not paid for or controlled by the seller.
Composition	An out-of-court settlement in which creditors agree to accept a fractional settlement on their original claim is referred to as composition.
Negotiation	Negotiation is the process whereby interested parties resolve disputes, agree upon courses of action, bargain for individual or collective advantage, and/or attempt to craft outcomes which serve their mutual interests.
Inception	The date and time on which coverage under an insurance policy takes effect is inception. Also refers to the date at which a stock or mutual fund was first traded.
Anticipation	In finance, anticipation is where debts are paid off early, generally in order to pay less interest.
Civil service	A collective term for all nonmilitary employees of a government. Paramilitary organizations, such as police and firefighters, are always included in civil service counts in the United States. Civil service employment is not the same as merit system employment, because all patronage positions are included in civil service totals.
Statute	A statute is a formal, written law of a country or state, written and enacted by its legislative authority, perhaps to then be ratified by the highest executive in the government, and finally published.
Legal system	Legal system refers to system of rules that regulate behavior and the processes by which the laws of a country are enforced and through which redress of grievances is obtained.
Hearing	A hearing is a proceeding before a court or other decision-making body or officer. A hearing is generally distinguished from a trial in that it is usually shorter and often less formal.

Go to **Cram101.com** for the Practice Tests for this Chapter.

Chapter 4. BASIC PRINCIPLES AND ORGANIZATION OF THE UNITED NATIONS

Chapter 5. BASIC STRUCTURE AND OPERATIONS OF THE UNITED NATIONS

Interest	In finance and economics, interest is the price paid by a borrower for the use of a lender's money. In other words, interest is the amount of paid to "rent" money for a period of time.
Warrant	A warrant is a security that entitles the holder to buy or sell a certain additional quantity of an underlying security at an agreed-upon price, at the holder's discretion.
United Nations	An international organization created by multilateral treaty in 1945 to promote social and economic cooperation among nations and to protect human rights is the United Nations.
Power center	A huge shopping strip with a multiple anchor, a convenient location, and a supermarket is called power center.
Covenant	A covenant is a signed written agreement between two or more parties. Also referred to as a contract.
Charter	Charter refers to an instrument or authority from the sovereign power bestowing the right or power to do business under the corporate form of organization. Also, the organic law of a city or town, and representing a portion of the statute law of the state.
Service	Service refers to a "non tangible product" that is not embodied in a physical good and that typically effects some change in another product, person, or institution. Contrasts with good.
Cooperative	A business owned and controlled by the people who use it, producers, consumers, or workers with similar needs who pool their resources for mutual gain is called cooperative.
Sovereignty	A country or region's power and ability to rule itself and manage its own affairs. Some feel that membership in international organizations such as the WTO is a threat to their sovereignty.
Concession	A concession is a business operated under a contract or license associated with a degree of exclusivity in exploiting a business within a certain geographical area. For example, sports arenas or public parks may have concession stands; and public services such as water supply may be operated as concessions.
Union	A worker association that bargains with employers over wages and working conditions is called a union.
Termination	The ending of a corporation that occurs only after the winding-up of the corporation's affairs, the liquidation of its assets, and the distribution of the proceeds to the claimants are referred to as a termination.
Security	Security refers to a claim on the borrower future income that is sold by the borrower to the lender. A security is a type of transferable interest representing financial value.
Channel	Channel, in communications (sometimes called communications channel), refers to the medium used to convey information from a sender (or transmitter) to a receiver.
Treaties	The first source of international law, consisting of agreements or contracts between two or more nations that are formally signed by an authorized representative and ratified by the supreme power of each nation are called treaties.
Grant	Grant refers to an intergovernmental transfer of funds. Since the New Deal, state and local governments have become increasingly dependent upon federal grants for an almost infinite variety of programs.
Committee	A long-lasting, sometimes permanent team in the organization structure created to deal with tasks that recur regularly is the committee.
Compromise	Compromise occurs when the interaction is moderately important to meeting goals and the goals are neither completely compatible nor completely incompatible.

Chapter 5. BASIC STRUCTURE AND OPERATIONS OF THE UNITED NATIONS

Chapter 5. BASIC STRUCTURE AND OPERATIONS OF THE UNITED NATIONS

Expense	In accounting, an expense represents an event in which an asset is used up or a liability is incurred. In terms of the accounting equation, expenses reduce owners' equity.
Budget	Budget refers to an account, usually for a year, of the planned expenditures and the expected receipts of an entity. For a government, the receipts are tax revenues.
Policy	Similar to a script in that a policy can be a less than completely rational decision-making method. Involves the use of a pre-existing set of decision steps for any problem that presents itself.
Journal	Book of original entry, in which transactions are recorded in a general ledger system, is referred to as a journal.
International law	Law that governs affairs between nations and that regulates transactions between individuals and businesses of different countries is an international law.
Trend	Trend refers to the long-term movement of an economic variable, such as its average rate of increase or decrease over enough years to encompass several business cycles.
Complaint	The pleading in a civil case in which the plaintiff states his claim and requests relief is called complaint. In the common law, it is a formal legal document that sets out the basic facts and legal reasons that the filing party (the plaintiffs) believes are sufficient to support a claim against another person, persons, entity or entities (the defendants) that entitles the plaintiff(s) to a remedy (either money damages or injunctive relief).
Delegation	Delegation is the handing of a task over to another person, usually a subordinate. It is the assignment of authority and responsibility to another person to carry out specific activities.
Subsidiary	A company that is controlled by another company or corporation is a subsidiary.
Personnel	A collective term for all of the employees of an organization. Personnel is also commonly used to refer to the personnel management function or the organizational unit responsible for administering personnel programs.
Staffing	Staffing refers to a management function that includes hiring, motivating, and retaining the best people available to accomplish the company's objectives.
Closing	The finalization of a real estate sales transaction that passes title to the property from the seller to the buyer is referred to as a closing. Closing is a sales term which refers to the process of making a sale. It refers to reaching the final step, which may be an exchange of money or acquiring a signature.
Negotiation	Negotiation is the process whereby interested parties resolve disputes, agree upon courses of action, bargain for individual or collective advantage, and/or attempt to craft outcomes which serve their mutual interests.
Assignment	A transfer of property or some right or interest is referred to as assignment.
Public relations	Public relations refers to the management function that evaluates public attitudes, changes policies and procedures in response to the public's requests, and executes a program of action and information to earn public understanding and acceptance.
Administration	Administration refers to the management and direction of the affairs of governments and institutions; a collective term for all policymaking officials of a government; the execution and implementation of public policy.
Specialist	A specialist is a trader who makes a market in one or several stocks and holds the limit order book for those stocks.
Protocol	Protocol refers to a statement that, before product development begins, identifies a well-

Chapter 5. BASIC STRUCTURE AND OPERATIONS OF THE UNITED NATIONS

Chapter 5. BASIC STRUCTURE AND OPERATIONS OF THE UNITED NATIONS

	defined target market; specific customers' needs, wants, and preferences; and what the product will be and do.
Liaison	An individual who serves as a bridge between groups, tying groups together and facilitating the communication flow needed to integrate group activities is a liaison.
Economic development	Increase in the economic standard of living of a country's population, normally accomplished by increasing its stocks of physical and human capital and improving its technology is an economic development.
Capital	Capital generally refers to financial wealth, especially that used to start or maintain a business. In classical economics, capital is one of four factors of production, the others being land and labor and entrepreneurship.
Inputs	The inputs used by a firm or an economy are the labor, raw materials, electricity and other resources it uses to produce its outputs.
World Health Organization	The World Health Organization is a specialized agency of the United Nations, acting as a coordinating authority on international public health, headquartered in Geneva, Switzerland. It's constitution states that its mission "is the attainment by all peoples of the highest possible level of health". Its major task is to combat disease, especially key infectious diseases, and to promote the general health of the peoples of the world.
Balance	In banking and accountancy, the outstanding balance is the amount of money owned, (or due), that remains in a deposit account (or a loan account) at a given date, after all past remittances, payments and withdrawal have been accounted for. It can be positive (then, in the balance sheet of a firm, it is an asset) or negative (a liability).
Adoption	In corporation law, a corporation's acceptance of a pre-incorporation contract by action of its board of directors, by which the corporation becomes liable on the contract, is referred to as adoption.
Exchange	The trade of things of value between buyer and seller so that each is better off after the trade is called the exchange.
Boycott	To protest by refusing to purchase from someone, or otherwise do business with them. In international trade, a boycott most often takes the form of refusal to import a country's goods.
Principal	In agency law, one under whose direction an agent acts and for whose benefit that agent acts is a principal.
Tactic	A short-term immediate decision that, in its totality, leads to the achievement of strategic goals is called a tactic.
Abandonment	Abandonment in law, is the relinquishment of an interest, claim, privilege or possession. This broad meaning has a number of applications in different branches of law.
Preponderance	Preponderance of the evidence means that evidence, in the judgment of the juror, is entitled to the greatest weight, appears to be more credible, has greater force, and overcomes not only the opposing presumptions, but also the opposing evidence.
Prerogative	Prerogative refers to a special power, privilege, or immunity, usually used in reference to an official or his office.
Contribution	In business organization law, the cash or property contributed to a business by its owners is referred to as contribution.
World Bank	The World Bank is a group of five international organizations responsible for providing finance and advice to countries for the purposes of economic development and poverty reduction, and for encouraging and safeguarding international investment.

Chapter 5. BASIC STRUCTURE AND OPERATIONS OF THE UNITED NATIONS

Chapter 5. BASIC STRUCTURE AND OPERATIONS OF THE UNITED NATIONS

Corporation	A legal entity chartered by a state or the Federal government that is distinct and separate from the individuals who own it is a corporation. This separation gives the corporation unique powers which other legal entities lack.
Fund	Independent accounting entity with a self-balancing set of accounts segregated for the purposes of carrying on specific activities is referred to as a fund.
International Monetary Fund	The International Monetary Fund is the international organization entrusted with overseeing the global financial system by monitoring exchange rates and balance of payments, as well as offering technical and financial assistance when asked.
Leadership	Management merely consists of leadership applied to business situations; or in other words: management forms a sub-set of the broader process of leadership.
Objection	In the trial of a case the formal remonstrance made by counsel to something that has been said or done, in order to obtain the court's ruling thereon is an objection.
Accommodation	Accommodation is a term used to describe a delivery of nonconforming goods meant as a partial performance of a contract for the sale of goods, where a full performance is not possible.
Promotion	Promotion refers to all the techniques sellers use to motivate people to buy products or services. An attempt by marketers to inform people about products and to persuade them to participate in an exchange.
Structural adjustment	Structural adjustment is a term used by the International Monetary Fund for the changes it recommends for developing countries. These changes are designed to promote economic growth, to generate income, to pay off the debt which the countries have accumulated.
Solvency	The ability of a company to pay interest as it comes due and to repay the face value of debt at maturity is called solvency.
Assessment	Collecting information and providing feedback to employees about their behavior, communication style, or skills is an assessment.
Asset	An item of property, such as land, capital, money, a share in ownership, or a claim on others for future payment, such as a bond or a bank deposit is an asset.
Operation	A standardized method or technique that is performed repetitively, often on different materials resulting in different finished goods is called an operation.
Financial crisis	A loss of confidence in a country's currency or other financial assets causing international investors to withdraw their funds from the country is referred to as a financial crisis.
Authority	Authority in agency law, refers to an agent's ability to affect his principal's legal relations with third parties. Also used to refer to an actor's legal power or ability to do something. In addition, sometimes used to refer to a statute, case, or other legal source that justifies a particular result.
Endowment	Endowment refers to the amount of something that a person or country simply has, rather than their having somehow to acquire it.
Working capital	The dollar difference between total current assets and total current liabilities is called working capital.
Bond	Bond refers to a debt instrument, issued by a borrower and promising a specified stream of payments to the purchaser, usually regular interest payments plus a final repayment of principal.
Purchasing	Purchasing refers to the function in a firm that searches for quality material resources, finds the best suppliers, and negotiates the best price for goods and services.
Pledge	In law a pledge (also pawn) is a bailment of personal property as a security for some debt or

Chapter 5. BASIC STRUCTURE AND OPERATIONS OF THE UNITED NATIONS

Chapter 5. BASIC STRUCTURE AND OPERATIONS OF THE UNITED NATIONS

	engagement.
Budget deficit	A budget deficit occurs when an entity (often a government) spends more money than it takes
Deficit	The deficit is the amount by which expenditure exceed revenue.
Strike	The withholding of labor services by an organized group of workers is referred to as a strike.
Short run	Short run refers to a period of time that permits an increase or decrease in current production volume with existing capacity, but one that is too short to permit enlargement of that capacity itself (eg, the building of new plants, training of additional workers, etc.).
American Bar Association	The American Bar Association is a voluntary bar association of lawyers and law students, which is not specific to any jurisdiction in the United States. The most important activities are the setting of academic standards for law schools, and the formulation of model legal codes.
Legislative branch	The part of the government that consists of Congress and has the power to adopt laws is called the legislative branch.
Foundation	A Foundation is a type of philanthropic organization set up by either individuals or institutions as a legal entity (either as a corporation or trust) with the purpose of distributing grants to support causes in line with the goals of the foundation.
Ford	Ford is an American company that manufactures and sells automobiles worldwide. Ford introduced methods for large-scale manufacturing of cars, and large-scale management of an industrial workforce, especially elaborately engineered manufacturing sequences typified by the moving assembly lines.
Rule of law	A legal system in which rules are clear, well-understood, and fairly enforced, including property rights and enforcement of contracts is called rule of law.
Bankruptcy	Bankruptcy is a legally declared inability or impairment of ability of an individual or organization to pay their creditors.
Revenue	Revenue is a U.S. business term for the amount of money that a company receives from its activities, mostly from sales of products and/or services to customers.
Jurisdiction	The power of a court to hear and decide a case is called jurisdiction. It is the practical authority granted to a formally constituted body or to a person to deal with and make pronouncements on legal matters and, by implication, to administer justice within a defined area of responsibility.
Licensing	Licensing is a form of strategic alliance which involves the sale of a right to use certain proprietary knowledge (so called intellectual property) in a defined way.
Aid	Assistance provided by countries and by international institutions such as the World Bank to developing countries in the form of monetary grants, loans at low interest rates, in kind, or a combination of these is called aid. Aid can also refer to assistance of any type rendered to benefit some group or individual.

Chapter 5. BASIC STRUCTURE AND OPERATIONS OF THE UNITED NATIONS

Chapter 6. PEACEFUL SETTLEMENT OF DISPUTES

United Nations	An international organization created by multilateral treaty in 1945 to promote social and economic cooperation among nations and to protect human rights is the United Nations.
Long run	In economic models, the long run time frame assumes no fixed factors of production. Firms can enter or leave the marketplace, and the cost (and availability) of land, labor, raw materials, and capital goods can be assumed to vary.
Covenant	A covenant is a signed written agreement between two or more parties. Also referred to as a contract.
Charter	Charter refers to an instrument or authority from the sovereign power bestowing the right or power to do business under the corporate form of organization. Also, the organic law of a city or town, and representing a portion of the statute law of the state.
Security	Security refers to a claim on the borrower future income that is sold by the borrower to the lender. A security is a type of transferable interest representing financial value.
Frequency	Frequency refers to the speed of the up and down movements of a fluctuating economic variable; that is, the number of times per unit of time that the variable completes a cycle of up and down movement.
Conflict resolution	Conflict resolution is the process of resolving a dispute or a conflict. Successful conflict resolution occurs by providing each side's needs, and adequately addressing their interests so that they are each satisfied with the outcome. Conflict resolution aims to end conflicts before they start or lead to physical fighting.
Incentive	An incentive is any factor (financial or non-financial) that provides a motive for a particular course of action, or counts as a reason for preferring one choice to the alternatives.
Prerogative	Prerogative refers to a special power, privilege, or immunity, usually used in reference to an official or his office.
Sovereignty	A country or region's power and ability to rule itself and manage its own affairs. Some feel that membership in international organizations such as the WTO is a threat to their sovereignty.
Conciliation	A form of mediation in which the parties choose an interested third party to act as the mediator is referred to as conciliation.
Negotiation	Negotiation is the process whereby interested parties resolve disputes, agree upon courses of action, bargain for individual or collective advantage, and/or attempt to craft outcomes which serve their mutual interests.
Arbitration	Arbitration is a form of mediation or conciliation, where the mediating party is given power by the disputant parties to settle the dispute by making a finding. In practice arbitration is generally used as a substitute for judicial systems, particularly when the judicial processes are viewed as too slow, expensive or biased. Arbitration is also used by communities which lack formal law, as a substitute for formal law.
Mediation	Mediation consists of a process of alternative dispute resolution in which a (generally) neutral third party using appropriate techniques, assists two or more parties to help them negotiate an agreement, with concrete effects, on a matter of common interest.
Option	A contract that gives the purchaser the option to buy or sell the underlying financial instrument at a specified price, called the exercise price or strike price, within a specific period of time.
Compromise	Compromise occurs when the interaction is moderately important to meeting goals and the goals are neither completely compatible nor completely incompatible.

Chapter 6. PEACEFUL SETTLEMENT OF DISPUTES

Chapter 6. PEACEFUL SETTLEMENT OF DISPUTES

Aid	Assistance provided by countries and by international institutions such as the World Bank to developing countries in the form of monetary grants, loans at low interest rates, in kind, or a combination of these is called aid. Aid can also refer to assistance of any type rendered to benefit some group or individual.
Investment	Investment refers to spending for the production and accumulation of capital and additions to inventories. In a financial sense, buying an asset with the expectation of making a return.
Trade dispute	Trade dispute refers to any disagreement between nations involving their international trade or trade policies.
Statute	A statute is a formal, written law of a country or state, written and enacted by its legislative authority, perhaps to then be ratified by the highest executive in the government, and finally published.
Consideration	Consideration in contract law, a basic requirement for an enforceable agreement under traditional contract principles, defined in this text as legal value, bargained for and given in exchange for an act or promise. In corporation law, cash or property contributed to a corporation in exchange for shares, or a promise to contribute such cash or property.
Adoption	In corporation law, a corporation's acceptance of a pre-incorporation contract by action of its board of directors, by which the corporation becomes liable on the contract, is referred to as adoption.
Jurisdiction	The power of a court to hear and decide a case is called jurisdiction. It is the practical authority granted to a formally constituted body or to a person to deal with and make pronouncements on legal matters and, by implication, to administer justice within a defined area of responsibility.
Domestic	From or in one's own country. A domestic producer is one that produces inside the home country. A domestic price is the price inside the home country. Opposite of 'foreign' or 'world.'.
Gain	In finance, gain is a profit or an increase in value of an investment such as a stock or bond. Gain is calculated by fair market value or the proceeds from the sale of the investment minus the sum of the purchase price and all costs associated with it.
Aggrieved	Aggrieved refers to one whose legal rights have been invaded by the act of another. Also, one whose pecuniary interest is directly affected by a judgment, or whose right of property may be divested by an action.
Agent	A person who makes economic decisions for another economic actor. A hired manager operates as an agent for a firm's owner.
Final settlement	Final settlement occurs when the payor bank pays the check in cash, settles for the check without having a right to revoke the settlement, or fails to dishonor the check within certain statutory time periods.
Trend	Trend refers to the long-term movement of an economic variable, such as its average rate of increase or decrease over enough years to encompass several business cycles.
Contribution	In business organization law, the cash or property contributed to a business by its owners is referred to as contribution.
Case study	A case study is a particular method of qualitative research. Rather than using large samples and following a rigid protocol to examine a limited number of variables, case study methods involve an in-depth, longitudinal examination of a single instance or event: a case. They provide a systematic way of looking at events, collecting data, analyzing information, and reporting the results.

Go to Cram101.com for the Practice Tests for this Chapter.

Chapter 6. PEACEFUL SETTLEMENT OF DISPUTES

Chapter 6. PEACEFUL SETTLEMENT OF DISPUTES

Personnel	A collective term for all of the employees of an organization. Personnel is also commonly used to refer to the personnel management function or the organizational unit responsible for administering personnel programs.
Complaint	The pleading in a civil case in which the plaintiff states his claim and requests relief is called complaint. In the common law, it is a formal legal document that sets out the basic facts and legal reasons that the filing party (the plaintiffs) believes are sufficient to support a claim against another person, persons, entity or entities (the defendants) that entitles the plaintiff(s) to a remedy (either money damages or injunctive relief).
Brief	Brief refers to a statement of a party's case or legal arguments, usually prepared by an attorney. Also used to make legal arguments before appellate courts.
Points	Loan origination fees that may be deductible as interest by a buyer of property. A seller of property who pays points reduces the selling price by the amount of the points paid for the buyer.
Coercion	Economic coercion is when an agent puts economic pressure onto the victim. The most common example of this is cutting off the supply to an essential resource, such as water.
Publicity	Publicity refers to any information about an individual, product, or organization that's distributed to the public through the media and that's not paid for or controlled by the seller.
Appeal	Appeal refers to the act of asking an appellate court to overturn a decision after the trial court's final judgment has been entered.
Union	A worker association that bargains with employers over wages and working conditions is called a union.
Per capita	Per capita refers to per person. Usually used to indicate the average per person of any given statistic, commonly income.
Per capita income	The per capita income for a group of people may be defined as their total personal income, divided by the total population. Per capita income is usually reported in units of currency per year.
Authority	Authority in agency law, refers to an agent's ability to affect his principal's legal relations with third parties. Also used to refer to an actor's legal power or ability to do something. In addition, sometimes used to refer to a statute, case, or other legal source that justifies a particular result.
Economic problem	Economic problem refers to how to determine the use of scarce resources among competing uses. Because resources are scarce, the economy must choose what products to produce; how these products are to be produced: and for whom.
Trustee	An independent party appointed to represent the bondholders is referred to as a trustee.
Assignment	A transfer of property or some right or interest is referred to as assignment.
Verification	Verification refers to the final stage of the creative process where the validity or truthfulness of the insight is determined. The feedback portion of communication in which the receiver sends a message to the source indicating receipt of the message and the degree to which he or she understood the message.
Accession	Accession refers to the process of adding a country to an international agreement, such as the GATT, WTO, EU, or NAFTA.
Holding	The holding is a court's determination of a matter of law based on the issue presented in the particular case. In other words: under this law, with these facts, this result.

Chapter 6. PEACEFUL SETTLEMENT OF DISPUTES

Administrator	Administrator refers to the personal representative appointed by a probate court to settle the estate of a deceased person who died.
Points of difference	Those characteristics of a product that make it superior to competitive substitutes are points of difference.
Integration	Economic integration refers to reducing barriers among countries to transactions and to movements of goods, capital, and labor, including harmonization of laws, regulations, and standards. Integrated markets theoretically function as a unified market.
Prime minister	The Prime Minister of the United Kingdom of Great Britain and Northern Ireland is the head of government and so exercises many of the executive functions nominally vested in the Sovereign, who is head of state. According to custom, the Prime Minister and the Cabinet (which he or she heads) are accountable for their actions to Parliament, of which they are members by (modern) convention.
Remainder	A remainder in property law is a future interest created in a transferee that is capable of becoming possessory upon the natural termination of a prior estate created by the same instrument.
Incorporation	Incorporation is the forming of a new corporation. The corporation may be a business, a non-profit organization or even a government of a new city or town.
Policy	Similar to a script in that a policy can be a less than completely rational decision-making method. Involves the use of a pre-existing set of decision steps for any problem that presents itself.
Enterprise	Enterprise refers to another name for a business organization. Other similar terms are business firm, sometimes simply business, sometimes simply firm, as well as company, and entity.
Labor	People's physical and mental talents and efforts that are used to help produce goods and services are called labor.
Standard of living	Standard of living refers to the level of consumption that people enjoy, on the average, and is measured by average income per person.
Treaties	The first source of international law, consisting of agreements or contracts between two or more nations that are formally signed by an authorized representative and ratified by the supreme power of each nation are called treaties.
Committee	A long-lasting, sometimes permanent team in the organization structure created to deal with tasks that recur regularly is the committee.
Delegation	Delegation is the handing of a task over to another person, usually a subordinate. It is the assignment of authority and responsibility to another person to carry out specific activities.
Export	In economics, an export is any good or commodity, shipped or otherwise transported out of a country, province, town to another part of the world in a legitimate fashion, typically for use in trade or sale.
Embargo	Embargo refers to the prohibition of some category of trade. May apply to exports and/or imports, of particular products or of all trade, vis a vis the world or a particular country or countries.
Argument	The discussion by counsel for the respective parties of their contentions on the law and the facts of the case being tried in order to aid the jury in arriving at a correct and just conclusion is called argument.
Principal	In agency law, one under whose direction an agent acts and for whose benefit that agent acts

Chapter 6. PEACEFUL SETTLEMENT OF DISPUTES

Chapter 6. PEACEFUL SETTLEMENT OF DISPUTES

	is a principal.
Pledge	In law a pledge (also pawn) is a bailment of personal property as a security for some debt or engagement.
Margin	A deposit by a buyer in stocks with a seller or a stockbroker, as security to cover fluctuations in the market in reference to stocks that the buyer has purchased but for which he has not paid is a margin. Commodities are also traded on margin.
Boycott	To protest by refusing to purchase from someone, or otherwise do business with them. In international trade, a boycott most often takes the form of refusal to import a country's goods.
Balance	In banking and accountancy, the outstanding balance is the amount of money owned, (or due), that remains in a deposit account (or a loan account) at a given date, after all past remittances, payments and withdrawal have been accounted for. It can be positive (then, in the balance sheet of a firm, it is an asset) or negative (a liability).
Ad hoc	Ad hoc is a Latin phrase which means "for this purpose." It generally signifies a solution that has been tailored to a specific purpose and is makeshift and non-general, such as a handcrafted network protocol or a specific-purpose equation, as opposed to general solutions.
Interest	In finance and economics, interest is the price paid by a borrower for the use of a lender's money. In other words, interest is the amount of paid to "rent" money for a period of time.
Intervention	Intervention refers to an activity in which a government buys or sells its currency in the foreign exchange market in order to affect its currency's exchange rate.
Instrument	Instrument refers to an economic variable that is controlled by policy makers and can be used to influence other variables, called targets. Examples are monetary and fiscal policies used to achieve external and internal balance.
Credibility	The extent to which a source is perceived as having knowledge, skill, or experience relevant to a communication topic and can be trusted to give an unbiased opinion or present objective information on the issue is called credibility.
Takeover	A takeover in business refers to one company (the acquirer) purchasing another (the target). Such events resemble mergers, but without the formation of a new company.
Assessment	Collecting information and providing feedback to employees about their behavior, communication style, or skills is an assessment.
Asset	An item of property, such as land, capital, money, a share in ownership, or a claim on others for future payment, such as a bond or a bank deposit is an asset.
Grant	Grant refers to an intergovernmental transfer of funds . Since the New Deal, state and local governments have become increasingly dependent upon federal grants for an almost infinite variety of programs.
Compliance	A type of influence process where a receiver accepts the position advocated by a source to obtain favorable outcomes or to avoid punishment is the compliance.
Leadership	Management merely consists of leadership applied to business situations; or in other words: management forms a sub-set of the broader process of leadership.
Economy	The income, expenditures, and resources that affect the cost of running a business and household are called an economy.
Service	Service refers to a "non tangible product" that is not embodied in a physical good and that typically effects some change in another product, person, or institution. Contrasts with good.

Chapter 6. PEACEFUL SETTLEMENT OF DISPUTES

Chapter 6. PEACEFUL SETTLEMENT OF DISPUTES

Division of labor	Division of labor is generally speaking the specialization of cooperative labor in specific, circumscribed tasks and roles, intended to increase efficiency of output.
Cooperative	A business owned and controlled by the people who use it, producers, consumers, or workers with similar needs who pool their resources for mutual gain is called cooperative.
Channel	Channel, in communications (sometimes called communications channel), refers to the medium used to convey information from a sender (or transmitter) to a receiver.
Innovation	Innovation refers to the first commercially successful introduction of a new product, the use of a new method of production, or the creation of a new form of business organization.
Accommodation	Accommodation is a term used to describe a delivery of nonconforming goods meant as a partial performance of a contract for the sale of goods, where a full performance is not possible.
Comprehensive	A comprehensive refers to a layout accurate in size, color, scheme, and other necessary details to show how a final ad will look. For presentation only, never for reproduction.
Utility	Utility refers to the want-satisfying power of a good or service; the satisfaction or pleasure a consumer obtains from the consumption of a good or service.
Dividend	Amount of corporate profits paid out for each share of stock is referred to as dividend.
Welfare	Welfare refers to the economic well being of an individual, group, or economy. For individuals, it is conceptualized by a utility function. For groups, including countries and the world, it is a tricky philosophical concept, since individuals fare differently.

Go to **Cram101.com** for the Practice Tests for this Chapter.

Chapter 6. PEACEFUL SETTLEMENT OF DISPUTES

Chapter 7. COLLECTIVE SECURITY AND ITS ALTERNATIVES: THEORY AND PRACTICE

United Nations	An international organization created by multilateral treaty in 1945 to promote social and economic cooperation among nations and to protect human rights is the United Nations.
Principal	In agency law, one under whose direction an agent acts and for whose benefit that agent acts is a principal.
Channel	Channel, in communications (sometimes called communications channel), refers to the medium used to convey information from a sender (or transmitter) to a receiver.
Security	Security refers to a claim on the borrower future income that is sold by the borrower to the lender. A security is a type of transferable interest representing financial value.
Credit	Credit refers to a recording as positive in the balance of payments, any transaction that gives rise to a payment into the country, such as an export, the sale of an asset, or borrowing from abroad.
Balance	In banking and accountancy, the outstanding balance is the amount of money owned, (or due), that remains in a deposit account (or a loan account) at a given date, after all past remittances, payments and withdrawal have been accounted for. It can be positive (then, in the balance sheet of a firm, it is an asset) or negative (a liability).
Sovereignty	A country or region's power and ability to rule itself and manage its own affairs. Some feel that membership in international organizations such as the WTO is a threat to their sovereignty.
Interest	In finance and economics, interest is the price paid by a borrower for the use of a lender's money. In other words, interest is the amount of paid to "rent" money for a period of time.
Contribution	In business organization law, the cash or property contributed to a business by its owners is referred to as contribution.
Liability	A liability is a present obligation of the enterprise arizing from past events, the settlement of which is expected to result in an outflow from the enterprise of resources embodying economic benefits.
Investment	Investment refers to spending for the production and accumulation of capital and additions to inventories. In a financial sense, buying an asset with the expectation of making a return.
Leadership	Management merely consists of leadership applied to business situations; or in other words: management forms a sub-set of the broader process of leadership.
Covenant	A covenant is a signed written agreement between two or more parties. Also referred to as a contract.
Prohibition	Prohibition refers to denial of the right to import or export, applying to particular products and/or particular countries. Includes embargo.
Ipso facto	Ipso facto is a Latin phrase, directly translated as by that very fact.
Economic sanction	A economic sanction can vary from imposing import duties on goods from, or blocking the export of certain goods to the target country, to a full naval blockade of its ports in an effort to verify, and curb or block specified imported goods.
Embargo	Embargo refers to the prohibition of some category of trade. May apply to exports and/or imports, of particular products or of all trade, vis a vis the world or a particular country or countries.
Aid	Assistance provided by countries and by international institutions such as the World Bank to developing countries in the form of monetary grants, loans at low interest rates, in kind, or a combination of these is called aid. Aid can also refer to assistance of any type rendered to benefit some group or individual.

Chapter 7. COLLECTIVE SECURITY AND ITS ALTERNATIVES: THEORY AND PRACTICE

Chapter 7. COLLECTIVE SECURITY AND ITS ALTERNATIVES: THEORY AND PRACTICE

Economy	The income, expenditures, and resources that affect the cost of running a business and household are called an economy.
Supply	Supply is the aggregate amount of any material good that can be called into being at a certain price point; it comprises one half of the equation of supply and demand. In classical economic theory, a curve representing supply is one of the factors that produce price.
Pact	Pact refers to a set of principles endorsed by 21 of the largest U.S. ad agencies aimed at improving the research used in preparing and testing ads, providing a better creative product for clients, and controlling the cost of TV commercials.
Expense	In accounting, an expense represents an event in which an asset is used up or a liability is incurred. In terms of the accounting equation, expenses reduce owners' equity.
Union	A worker association that bargains with employers over wages and working conditions is called a union.
Shell	One of the original Seven Sisters, Royal Dutch/Shell is the world's third-largest oil company by revenue, and a major player in the petrochemical industry and the solar energy business. Shell has six core businesses: Exploration and Production, Gas and Power, Downstream, Chemicals, Renewables, and Trading/Shipping, and operates in more than 140 countries.
Condemnation	The process whereby the government acquires the ownership of private property for a public use over the protest of the owner is called condemnation. It is identical to eminent domain.
Charter	Charter refers to an instrument or authority from the sovereign power bestowing the right or power to do business under the corporate form of organization. Also, the organic law of a city or town, and representing a portion of the statute law of the state.
Prerogative	Prerogative refers to a special power, privilege, or immunity, usually used in reference to an official or his office.
Negotiation	Negotiation is the process whereby interested parties resolve disputes, agree upon courses of action, bargain for individual or collective advantage, and/or attempt to craft outcomes which serve their mutual interests.
Standing	Standing refers to the legal requirement that anyone seeking to challenge a particular action in court must demonstrate that such action substantially affects his legitimate interests before he will be entitled to bring suit.
Committee	A long-lasting, sometimes permanent team in the organization structure created to deal with tasks that recur regularly is the committee.
Service	Service refers to a "non tangible product" that is not embodied in a physical good and that typically effects some change in another product, person, or institution. Contrasts with good.
Quota	A government-imposed restriction on quantity, or sometimes on total value, used to restrict the import of something to a specific quantity is called a quota.
Comprehensive	A comprehensive refers to a layout accurate in size, color, scheme, and other necessary details to show how a final ad will look. For presentation only, never for reproduction.
Authority	Authority in agency law, refers to an agent's ability to affect his principal's legal relations with third parties. Also used to refer to an actor's legal power or ability to do something. In addition, sometimes used to refer to a statute, case, or other legal source that justifies a particular result.
Adoption	In corporation law, a corporation's acceptance of a pre-incorporation contract by action of its board of directors, by which the corporation becomes liable on the contract, is referred to as adoption.

Chapter 7. COLLECTIVE SECURITY AND ITS ALTERNATIVES: THEORY AND PRACTICE

Chapter 7. COLLECTIVE SECURITY AND ITS ALTERNATIVES: THEORY AND PRACTICE

International law	Law that governs affairs between nations and that regulates transactions between individuals and businesses of different countries is an international law.
Agent	A person who makes economic decisions for another economic actor. A hired manager operates as an agent for a firm's owner.
Scope	Scope of a project is the sum total of all projects products and their requirements or features.
Grant	Grant refers to an intergovernmental transfer of funds. Since the New Deal, state and local governments have become increasingly dependent upon federal grants for an almost infinite variety of programs.
Instrument	Instrument refers to an economic variable that is controlled by policy makers and can be used to influence other variables, called targets. Examples are monetary and fiscal policies used to achieve external and internal balance.
Compliance	A type of influence process where a receiver accepts the position advocated by a source to obtain favorable outcomes or to avoid punishment is the compliance.
Exporting	Selling products to another country is called exporting.
Closing	The finalization of a real estate sales transaction that passes title to the property from the seller to the buyer is referred to as a closing. Closing is a sales term which refers to the process of making a sale. It refers to reaching the final step, which may be an exchange of money or acquiring a signature.
Innovation	Innovation refers to the first commercially successful introduction of a new product, the use of a new method of production, or the creation of a new form of business organization.
Personnel	A collective term for all of the employees of an organization. Personnel is also commonly used to refer to the personnel management function or the organizational unit responsible for administering personnel programs.
Conflict resolution	Conflict resolution is the process of resolving a dispute or a conflict. Successful conflict resolution occurs by providing each side's needs, and adequately addressing their interests so that they are each satisfied with the outcome. Conflict resolution aims to end conflicts before they start or lead to physical fighting.
Operation	A standardized method or technique that is performed repetitively, often on different materials resulting in different finished goods is called an operation.
Intervention	Intervention refers to an activity in which a government buys or sells its currency in the foreign exchange market in order to affect its currency's exchange rate.
Assignment	A transfer of property or some right or interest is referred to as assignment.
Policy	Similar to a script in that a policy can be a less than completely rational decision-making method. Involves the use of a pre-existing set of decision steps for any problem that presents itself.
Complement	A good that is used in conjunction with another good is a complement. For example, cameras and film would complement eachother.
Administration	Administration refers to the management and direction of the affairs of governments and institutions; a collective term for all policymaking officials of a government; the execution and implementation of public policy.
Conciliation	A form of mediation in which the parties choose an interested third party to act as the mediator is referred to as conciliation.
Budget	Budget refers to an account, usually for a year, of the planned expenditures and the expected

Chapter 7. COLLECTIVE SECURITY AND ITS ALTERNATIVES: THEORY AND PRACTICE

Chapter 7. COLLECTIVE SECURITY AND ITS ALTERNATIVES: THEORY AND PRACTICE

	receipts of an entity. For a government, the receipts are tax revenues.
Deficit	The deficit is the amount by which expenditure exceed revenue.
Financial crisis	A loss of confidence in a country's currency or other financial assets causing international investors to withdraw their funds from the country is referred to as a financial crisis.
Enterprise	Enterprise refers to another name for a business organization. Other similar terms are business firm, sometimes simply business, sometimes simply firm, as well as company, and entity.
Jurisdiction	The power of a court to hear and decide a case is called jurisdiction. It is the practical authority granted to a formally constituted body or to a person to deal with and make pronouncements on legal matters and, by implication, to administer justice within a defined area of responsibility.
Assessment	Collecting information and providing feedback to employees about their behavior, communication style, or skills is an assessment.
Specialist	A specialist is a trader who makes a market in one or several stocks and holds the limit order book for those stocks.
Boycott	To protest by refusing to purchase from someone, or otherwise do business with them. In international trade, a boycott most often takes the form of refusal to import a country's goods.
Incorporation	Incorporation is the forming of a new corporation. The corporation may be a business, a non-profit organization or even a government of a new city or town.
Capital	Capital generally refers to financial wealth, especially that used to start or maintain a business. In classical economics, capital is one of four factors of production, the others being land and labor and entrepreneurship.
Exchange	The trade of things of value between buyer and seller so that each is better off after the trade is called the exchange.
Final settlement	Final settlement occurs when the payor bank pays the check in cash, settles for the check without having a right to revoke the settlement, or fails to dishonor the check within certain statutory time periods.
Classical theory	The original theory about organizations that closely resembles military structures is called classical theory.
Credibility	The extent to which a source is perceived as having knowledge, skill, or experience relevant to a communication topic and can be trusted to give an unbiased opinion or present objective information on the issue is called credibility.
Complaint	The pleading in a civil case in which the plaintiff states his claim and requests relief is called complaint. In the common law, it is a formal legal document that sets out the basic facts and legal reasons that the filing party (the plaintiffs) believes are sufficient to support a claim against another person, persons, entity or entities (the defendants) that entitles the plaintiff(s) to a remedy (either money damages or injunctive relief).
Management	Management characterizes the process of leading and directing all or part of an organization, often a business, through the deployment and manipulation of resources. Early twentieth-century management writer Mary Parker Follett defined management as "the art of getting things done through people."
Controlling	A management function that involves determining whether or not an organization is progressing toward its goals and objectives, and taking corrective action if it is not is called controlling.

Chapter 7. COLLECTIVE SECURITY AND ITS ALTERNATIVES: THEORY AND PRACTICE

Chapter 7. COLLECTIVE SECURITY AND ITS ALTERNATIVES: THEORY AND PRACTICE

Brief	Brief refers to a statement of a party's case or legal arguments, usually prepared by an attorney. Also used to make legal arguments before appellate courts.
Inception	The date and time on which coverage under an insurance policy takes effect is inception. Also refers to the date at which a stock or mutual fund was first traded.
Affiliates	Local television stations that are associated with a major network are called affiliates. Affiliates agree to preempt time during specified hours for programming provided by the network and carry the advertising contained in the program.
Fund	Independent accounting entity with a self-balancing set of accounts segregated for the purposes of carrying on specific activities is referred to as a fund.
Holding	The holding is a court's determination of a matter of law based on the issue presented in the particular case. In other words: under this law, with these facts, this result.
Verification	Verification refers to the final stage of the creative process where the validity or truthfulness of the insight is determined. The feedback portion of communication in which the receiver sends a message to the source indicating receipt of the message and the degree to which he or she understood the message.
World Bank	The World Bank is a group of five international organizations responsible for providing finance and advice to countries for the purposes of economic development and poverty reduction, and for encouraging and safeguarding international investment.
Administrator	Administrator refers to the personal representative appointed by a probate court to settle the estate of a deceased person who died.
Host country	The country in which the parent-country organization seeks to locate or has already located a facility is a host country.
Bankruptcy	Bankruptcy is a legally declared inability or impairment of ability of an individual or organization to pay their creditors.
Conflict management	Conflict management refers to the long-term management of intractable conflicts. It is the label for the variety of ways by which people handle grievances -- standing up for what they consider to be right and against what they consider to be wrong.

Chapter 7. COLLECTIVE SECURITY AND ITS ALTERNATIVES: THEORY AND PRACTICE

Chapter 8. THE SEARCH FOR JUSTICE UNDER LAW

Customs	Customs is an authority or agency in a country responsible for collecting customs duties and for controlling the flow of people, animals and goods (including personal effects and hazardous items) in and out of the country.
United Nations	An international organization created by multilateral treaty in 1945 to promote social and economic cooperation among nations and to protect human rights is the United Nations.
International law	Law that governs affairs between nations and that regulates transactions between individuals and businesses of different countries is an international law.
Sovereignty	A country or region's power and ability to rule itself and manage its own affairs. Some feel that membership in international organizations such as the WTO is a threat to their sovereignty.
Legal system	Legal system refers to system of rules that regulate behavior and the processes by which the laws of a country are enforced and through which redress of grievances is obtained.
Compromise	Compromise occurs when the interaction is moderately important to meeting goals and the goals are neither completely compatible nor completely incompatible.
Authority	Authority in agency law, refers to an agent's ability to affect his principal's legal relations with third parties. Also used to refer to an actor's legal power or ability to do something. In addition, sometimes used to refer to a statute, case, or other legal source that justifies a particular result.
Regulation	Regulation refers to restrictions state and federal laws place on business with regard to the conduct of its activities.
Executive order	A legal rule issued by a chief executive usually pursuant to a delegation of power from the legislature is called executive order.
Compliance	A type of influence process where a receiver accepts the position advocated by a source to obtain favorable outcomes or to avoid punishment is the compliance.
Beneficiary	The person for whose benefit an insurance policy, trust, will, or contract is established is a beneficiary. In the case of a contract, the beneficiary is called a third-party beneficiary.
Trend	Trend refers to the long-term movement of an economic variable, such as its average rate of increase or decrease over enough years to encompass several business cycles.
Security	Security refers to a claim on the borrower future income that is sold by the borrower to the lender. A security is a type of transferable interest representing financial value.
Treaties	The first source of international law, consisting of agreements or contracts between two or more nations that are formally signed by an authorized representative and ratified by the supreme power of each nation are called treaties.
Ad hoc	Ad hoc is a Latin phrase which means "for this purpose." It generally signifies a solution that has been tailored to a specific purpose and is makeshift and non-general, such as a handcrafted network protocol or a specific-purpose equation, as opposed to general solutions.
Jurisdiction	The power of a court to hear and decide a case is called jurisdiction. It is the practical authority granted to a formally constituted body or to a person to deal with and make pronouncements on legal matters and, by implication, to administer justice within a defined area of responsibility.
Interest	In finance and economics, interest is the price paid by a borrower for the use of a lender's money. In other words, interest is the amount of paid to "rent" money for a period of time.
Assessment	Collecting information and providing feedback to employees about their behavior,

Chapter 8. THE SEARCH FOR JUSTICE UNDER LAW

Chapter 8. THE SEARCH FOR JUSTICE UNDER LAW

	communication style, or skills is an assessment.
Utility	Utility refers to the want-satisfying power of a good or service; the satisfaction or pleasure a consumer obtains from the consumption of a good or service.
Sources of international law	Those things that international tribunals rely on in settling international disputes are referred to as sources of international law.
Statutory law	State and federal constitutions, legislative enactments, treaties, and ordinances, in other words, written laws are referred to as statutory law.
Statute	A statute is a formal, written law of a country or state, written and enacted by its legislative authority, perhaps to then be ratified by the highest executive in the government, and finally published.
Gap	In December of 1995, Gap became the first major North American retailer to accept independent monitoring of the working conditions in a contract factory producing its garments. Gap is the largest specialty retailer in the United States.
Property	Assets defined in the broadest legal sense. Property includes the unrealized receivables of a cash basis taxpayer, but not services rendered.
Policy	Similar to a script in that a policy can be a less than completely rational decision-making method. Involves the use of a pre-existing set of decision steps for any problem that presents itself.
International trade	The export of goods and services from a country and the import of goods and services into a country is referred to as the international trade.
Reciprocity	An industrial buying practice in which two organizations agree to purchase each other's products and services is called reciprocity.
Arbitration	Arbitration is a form of mediation or conciliation, where the mediating party is given power by the disputant parties to settle the dispute by making a finding. In practice arbitration is generally used as a substitute for judicial systems, particularly when the judicial processes are viewed as too slow, expensive or biased. Arbitration is also used by communities which lack formal law, as a substitute for formal law.
Leadership	Management merely consists of leadership applied to business situations; or in other words: management forms a sub-set of the broader process of leadership.
Commerce	Commerce is the exchange of something of value between two entities. It is the central mechanism from which capitalism is derived.
Standing	Standing refers to the legal requirement that anyone seeking to challenge a particular action in court must demonstrate that such action substantially affects his legitimate interests before he will be entitled to bring suit.
Covenant	A covenant is a signed written agreement between two or more parties. Also referred to as a contract.
Budget	Budget refers to an account, usually for a year, of the planned expenditures and the expected receipts of an entity. For a government, the receipts are tax revenues.
Promotion	Promotion refers to all the techniques sellers use to motivate people to buy products or services. An attempt by marketers to inform people about products and to persuade them to participate in an exchange.
Sponsorship	When the advertiser assumes responsibility for the production and usually the content of a television program as well as the advertising that appears within it, we have sponsorship.

Go to Cram101.com for the Practice Tests for this Chapter.

Chapter 8. THE SEARCH FOR JUSTICE UNDER LAW

Chapter 8. THE SEARCH FOR JUSTICE UNDER LAW

Pact	Pact refers to a set of principles endorsed by 21 of the largest U.S. ad agencies aimed at improving the research used in preparing and testing ads, providing a better creative product for clients, and controlling the cost of TV commercials.
Instrument	Instrument refers to an economic variable that is controlled by policy makers and can be used to influence other variables, called targets. Examples are monetary and fiscal policies used to achieve external and internal balance.
Welfare	Welfare refers to the economic well being of an individual, group, or economy. For individuals, it is conceptualized by a utility function. For groups, including countries and the world, it is a tricky philosophical concept, since individuals fare differently.
Charter	Charter refers to an instrument or authority from the sovereign power bestowing the right or power to do business under the corporate form of organization. Also, the organic law of a city or town, and representing a portion of the statute law of the state.
Labor	People's physical and mental talents and efforts that are used to help produce goods and services are called labor.
Contribution	In business organization law, the cash or property contributed to a business by its owners is referred to as contribution.
Scope	Scope of a project is the sum total of all projects products and their requirements or features.
Credit	Credit refers to a recording as positive in the balance of payments, any transaction that gives rise to a payment into the country, such as an export, the sale of an asset, or borrowing from abroad.
Subsidiary	A company that is controlled by another company or corporation is a subsidiary.
Committee	A long-lasting, sometimes permanent team in the organization structure created to deal with tasks that recur regularly is the committee.
Frequency	Frequency refers to the speed of the up and down movements of a fluctuating economic variable; that is, the number of times per unit of time that the variable completes a cycle of up and down movement.
Customary international law	In addition to treaties and other expressed or ratified agreements that create international law, the International Court of Justice, legal scholars, jurists, the United Nations and its member states consider customary international law, coupled with General principles of law, to be primary sources of international law.
Principal	In agency law, one under whose direction an agent acts and for whose benefit that agent acts is a principal.
Privilege	Generally, a legal right to engage in conduct that would otherwise result in legal liability is a privilege. Privileges are commonly classified as absolute or conditional. Occasionally, privilege is also used to denote a legal right to refrain from particular behavior.
Domestic	From or in one's own country. A domestic producer is one that produces inside the home country. A domestic price is the price inside the home country. Opposite of 'foreign' or 'world.'.
Developed country	A developed country is one that enjoys a relatively high standard of living derived through an industrialized, diversified economy. Countries with a very high Human Development Index are generally considered developed countries.
Litigation	The process of bringing, maintaining, and defending a lawsuit is litigation.
Bad faith	A person's actual intent to mislead or deceive another is bad faith.

Chapter 8. THE SEARCH FOR JUSTICE UNDER LAW

Chapter 8. THE SEARCH FOR JUSTICE UNDER LAW

Peak	Peak refers to the point in the business cycle when an economic expansion reaches its highest point before turning down. Contrasts with trough.
Plaintiff	A plaintiff is the party who initiates a lawsuit (also known as an action) before a court. By doing so, the plaintiff seeks a legal remedy, and if successful, the court will issue judgment in favour of the plaintiff and make the appropriate court order.
Consideration	Consideration in contract law, a basic requirement for an enforceable agreement under traditional contract principles, defined in this text as legal value, bargained for and given in exchange for an act or promise. In corporation law, cash or property contributed to a corporation in exchange for shares, or a promise to contribute such cash or property.
Accretion	In finance, accretion is the change in the price of a bond bought at a discount between the original price and the par value of the bond.
Rule of law	A legal system in which rules are clear, well-understood, and fairly enforced, including property rights and enforcement of contracts is called rule of law.
Personnel	A collective term for all of the employees of an organization. Personnel is also commonly used to refer to the personnel management function or the organizational unit responsible for administering personnel programs.
Channel	Channel, in communications (sometimes called communications channel), refers to the medium used to convey information from a sender (or transmitter) to a receiver.
Objection	In the trial of a case the formal remonstrance made by counsel to something that has been said or done, in order to obtain the court's ruling thereon is an objection.
Damages	The sum of money recoverable by a plaintiff who has received a judgment in a civil case is called damages.
Configuration	An organization's shape, which reflects the division of labor and the means of coordinating the divided tasks is configuration.
Points	Loan origination fees that may be deductible as interest by a buyer of property. A seller of property who pays points reduces the selling price by the amount of the points paid for the buyer.
Annual report	An annual report is prepared by corporate management that presents financial information including financial statements, footnotes, and the management discussion and analysis.
Petition	A petition is a request to an authority, most commonly a government official or public entity. In the colloquial sense, a petition is a document addressed to some official and signed by numerous individuals.
Complaint	The pleading in a civil case in which the plaintiff states his claim and requests relief is called complaint. In the common law, it is a formal legal document that sets out the basic facts and legal reasons that the filing party (the plaintiffs) believes are sufficient to support a claim against another person, persons, entity or entities (the defendants) that entitles the plaintiff(s) to a remedy (either money damages or injunctive relief).
Prerogative	Prerogative refers to a special power, privilege, or immunity, usually used in reference to an official or his office.
Grant	Grant refers to an intergovernmental transfer of funds . Since the New Deal, state and local governments have become increasingly dependent upon federal grants for an almost infinite variety of programs.
Union	A worker association that bargains with employers over wages and working conditions is called a union.

Chapter 8. THE SEARCH FOR JUSTICE UNDER LAW

Chapter 8. THE SEARCH FOR JUSTICE UNDER LAW

International Atomic Energy Agency	International Atomic Energy Agency was established as an autonomous organization on July 29, 1957. It seeks to promote the peaceful use of nuclear energy and to inhibit its use for military purposes. United States President Dwight D. Eisenhower envisioned, in his "Atoms for Peace" speech before the UN General Assembly in 1953, the creation of this international body to control and develop the use of atomic energy.
Operation	A standardized method or technique that is performed repetitively, often on different materials resulting in different finished goods is called an operation.
Rationalization	Rationalization in economics is an attempt to change a pre-existing ad-hoc workflow into one that is based on a set of published rules.
Applicant	In many tribunal and administrative law suits, the person who initiates the claim is called the applicant.
Service	Service refers to a "non tangible product" that is not embodied in a physical good and that typically effects some change in another product, person, or institution. Contrasts with good.
Agent	A person who makes economic decisions for another economic actor. A hired manager operates as an agent for a firm's owner.
Accommodation	Accommodation is a term used to describe a delivery of nonconforming goods meant as a partial performance of a contract for the sale of goods, where a full performance is not possible.
Conflict of interest	A conflict that occurs when a corporate officer or director enters into a transaction with the corporation in which he or she has a personal interest is a conflict of interest.
Grand jury	A grand jury is a type of common law jury responsible for investigating alleged crimes, examining evidence, and issuing indictments if they believe that there is enough evidence for a trial to proceed. A grand jury is distinguished from a petit jury, which is used during trial; the names refer to their respective sizes (typically 25 and 12 members respectively).
Jury	A body of lay persons, selected by lot, or by some other fair and impartial means, to ascertain, under the guidance of the judge, the truth in questions of fact arising either in civil litigation or a criminal process is referred to as jury.
Contract	A contract is a "promise" or an "agreement" that is enforced or recognized by the law. In the civil law, a contract is considered to be part of the general law of obligations.
Fund	Independent accounting entity with a self-balancing set of accounts segregated for the purposes of carrying on specific activities is referred to as a fund.
Appeal	Appeal refers to the act of asking an appellate court to overturn a decision after the trial court's final judgment has been entered.
Concession	A concession is a business operated under a contract or license associated with a degree of exclusivity in exploiting a business within a certain geographical area. For example, sports arenas or public parks may have concession stands; and public services such as water supply may be operated as concessions.
Screening	Screening in economics refers to a strategy of combating adverse selection, one of the potential decision-making complications in cases of asymmetric information.
Composition	An out-of-court settlement in which creditors agree to accept a fractional settlement on their original claim is referred to as composition.
Standardization	Standardization, in the context related to technologies and industries, is the process of establishing a technical standard among competing entities in a market, where this will bring benefits without hurting competition.

Chapter 8. THE SEARCH FOR JUSTICE UNDER LAW

Chapter 8. THE SEARCH FOR JUSTICE UNDER LAW

Adoption	In corporation law, a corporation's acceptance of a pre-incorporation contract by action of its board of directors, by which the corporation becomes liable on the contract, is referred to as adoption.
Inter alia	Among other things is called inter alia.
Trial	An examination before a competent tribunal, according to the law of the land, of the facts or law put in issue in a cause, for the purpose of determining such issue is a trial. When the court hears and determines any issue of fact or law for the purpose of determining the rights of the parties, it may be considered a trial.
Draft	A signed, written order by which one party instructs another party to pay a specified sum to a third party, at sight or at a specific date is a draft.
Evaluation	The consumer's appraisal of the product or brand on important attributes is called evaluation.
Distortion	Distortion refers to any departure from the ideal of perfect competition that interferes with economic agents maximizing social welfare when they maximize their own.
Precedent	A previously decided court decision that is recognized as authority for the disposition of future decisions is a precedent.
Custody	The bare control or care of a thing as distinguished from the possession of it is called custody.
Jurisprudence	Jurisprudence is the theory and philosophy of law. Students of jurisprudence aim to understand the fundamental nature of law, and to analyze its purpose, structure, and application. Jurisprudential scholars (sometimes confusingly referred to as "jurists") hope to obtain a deeper understanding of the law, the kind of power that it exercises, and its role in human societies.
Globalization	The increasing world-wide integration of markets for goods, services and capital that attracted special attention in the late 1990s is called globalization.
Comprehensive	A comprehensive refers to a layout accurate in size, color, scheme, and other necessary details to show how a final ad will look. For presentation only, never for reproduction.
Immunity	Granted by law, immunity is the assurance that someone will be exempt from prosecution.
Appreciation	Appreciation refers to a rise in the value of a country's currency on the exchange market, relative either to a particular other currency or to a weighted average of other currencies. The currency is said to appreciate. Opposite of 'depreciation.' Appreciation can also refer to the increase in value of any asset.
International trade law	International trade law includes the appropriate rules and customs for handling trade between countries or between private companies across borders.
Conciliation	A form of mediation in which the parties choose an interested third party to act as the mediator is referred to as conciliation.
Inception	The date and time on which coverage under an insurance policy takes effect is inception. Also refers to the date at which a stock or mutual fund was first traded.
Investment	Investment refers to spending for the production and accumulation of capital and additions to inventories. In a financial sense, buying an asset with the expectation of making a return.
Labor law	Labor law is the body of laws, administrative rulings, and precedents which addresses the legal rights of, and restrictions on, workers and their organizations.
Corporation	A legal entity chartered by a state or the Federal government that is distinct and separate from the individuals who own it is a corporation. This separation gives the corporation

Go to Cram101.com for the Practice Tests for this Chapter.

Chapter 8. THE SEARCH FOR JUSTICE UNDER LAW

Chapter 8. THE SEARCH FOR JUSTICE UNDER LAW

	unique powers which other legal entities lack.
Futures	Futures refer to contracts for the sale and future delivery of stocks or commodities, wherein either party may waive delivery, and receive or pay, as the case may be, the difference in market price at the time set for delivery.
Endowment	Endowment refers to the amount of something that a person or country simply has, rather than their having somehow to acquire it.
American Bar Association	The American Bar Association is a voluntary bar association of lawyers and law students, which is not specific to any jurisdiction in the United States. The most important activities are the setting of academic standards for law schools, and the formulation of model legal codes.
Hearing	A hearing is a proceeding before a court or other decision-making body or officer. A hearing is generally distinguished from a trial in that it is usually shorter and often less formal.
Attachment	Attachment in general, the process of taking a person's property under an appropriate judicial order by an appropriate officer of the court. Used for a variety of purposes, including the acquisition of jurisdiction over the property seized and the securing of property that may be used to satisfy a debt.
Commercial law	The law that relates to the rights of property and persons engaged in trade or commerce and regulates corporate contracts, hiring practices, and the manufacture and sales of consumer goods is called commercial law.
Realization	Realization is the sale of assets when an entity is being liquidated.

Chapter 8. THE SEARCH FOR JUSTICE UNDER LAW

Chapter 9. CONTROLLING THE INSTRUMENTS OF WAR

Aid	Assistance provided by countries and by international institutions such as the World Bank to developing countries in the form of monetary grants, loans at low interest rates, in kind, or a combination of these is called aid. Aid can also refer to assistance of any type rendered to benefit some group or individual.
Controlling	A management function that involves determining whether or not an organization is progressing toward its goals and objectives, and taking corrective action if it is not is called controlling.
Instrument	Instrument refers to an economic variable that is controlled by policy makers and can be used to influence other variables, called targets. Examples are monetary and fiscal policies used to achieve external and internal balance.
Per capita	Per capita refers to per person. Usually used to indicate the average per person of any given statistic, commonly income.
Domestic	From or in one's own country. A domestic producer is one that produces inside the home country. A domestic price is the price inside the home country. Opposite of 'foreign' or 'world.'.
Gross domestic product	Gross domestic product refers to the total value of new goods and services produced in a given year within the borders of a country, regardless of by whom.
Budget	Budget refers to an account, usually for a year, of the planned expenditures and the expected receipts of an entity. For a government, the receipts are tax revenues.
Security	Security refers to a claim on the borrower future income that is sold by the borrower to the lender. A security is a type of transferable interest representing financial value.
Regulation	Regulation refers to restrictions state and federal laws place on business with regard to the conduct of its activities.
Incentive	An incentive is any factor (financial or non-financial) that provides a motive for a particular course of action, or counts as a reason for preferring one choice to the alternatives.
Firm	An organization that employs resources to produce a good or service for profit and owns and operates one or more plants is referred to as a firm.
Treaties	The first source of international law, consisting of agreements or contracts between two or more nations that are formally signed by an authorized representative and ratified by the supreme power of each nation are called treaties.
Covenant	A covenant is a signed written agreement between two or more parties. Also referred to as a contract.
Pledge	In law a pledge (also pawn) is a bailment of personal property as a security for some debt or engagement.
Production	The creation of finished goods and services using the factors of production: land, labor, capital, entrepreneurship, and knowledge.
Exchange	The trade of things of value between buyer and seller so that each is better off after the trade is called the exchange.
Industry	A group of firms that produce identical or similar products is an industry. It is also used specifically to refer to an area of economic production focused on manufacturing which involves large amounts of capital investment before any profit can be realized, also called "heavy industry".
Draft	A signed, written order by which one party instructs another party to pay a specified sum to

Chapter 9. CONTROLLING THE INSTRUMENTS OF WAR

Chapter 9. CONTROLLING THE INSTRUMENTS OF WAR

	a third party, at sight or at a specific date is a draft.
Gap	In December of 1995, Gap became the first major North American retailer to accept independent monitoring of the working conditions in a contract factory producing its garments. Gap is the largest specialty retailer in the United States.
Negotiation	Negotiation is the process whereby interested parties resolve disputes, agree upon courses of action, bargain for individual or collective advantage, and/or attempt to craft outcomes which serve their mutual interests.
Tangible	Having a physical existence is referred to as the tangible. Personal property other than real estate, such as cars, boats, stocks, or other assets.
Capital	Capital generally refers to financial wealth, especially that used to start or maintain a business. In classical economics, capital is one of four factors of production, the others being land and labor and entrepreneurship.
Abandonment	Abandonment in law, is the relinquishment of an interest, claim, privilege or possession. This broad meaning has a number of applications in different branches of law.
Prerogative	Prerogative refers to a special power, privilege, or immunity, usually used in reference to an official or his office.
Interest	In finance and economics, interest is the price paid by a borrower for the use of a lender's money. In other words, interest is the amount of paid to "rent" money for a period of time.
Gain	In finance, gain is a profit or an increase in value of an investment such as a stock or bond. Gain is calculated by fair market value or the proceeds from the sale of the investment minus the sum of the purchase price and all costs associated with it.
Policy	Similar to a script in that a policy can be a less than completely rational decision-making method. Involves the use of a pre-existing set of decision steps for any problem that presents itself.
Monopoly	A monopoly is defined as a persistent market situation where there is only one provider of a kind of product or service.
Union	A worker association that bargains with employers over wages and working conditions is called a union.
Leadership	Management merely consists of leadership applied to business situations; or in other words: management forms a sub-set of the broader process of leadership.
Channel	Channel, in communications (sometimes called communications channel), refers to the medium used to convey information from a sender (or transmitter) to a receiver.
Status quo	Status quo is a Latin term meaning the present, current, existing state of affairs.
Developing country	Developing country refers to a country whose per capita income is low by world standards. Same as LDC. As usually used, it does not necessarily connote that the country's income is rising.
Principal	In agency law, one under whose direction an agent acts and for whose benefit that agent acts is a principal.
Balance	In banking and accountancy, the outstanding balance is the amount of money owned, (or due), that remains in a deposit account (or a loan account) at a given date, after all past remittances, payments and withdrawal have been accounted for. It can be positive (then, in the balance sheet of a firm, it is an asset) or negative (a liability).
Authority	Authority in agency law, refers to an agent's ability to affect his principal's legal relations with third parties. Also used to refer to an actor's legal power or ability to do

Go to Cram101.com for the Practice Tests for this Chapter.

Chapter 9. CONTROLLING THE INSTRUMENTS OF WAR

Chapter 9. CONTROLLING THE INSTRUMENTS OF WAR

	something. In addition, sometimes used to refer to a statute, case, or other legal source that justifies a particular result.
Sovereignty	A country or region's power and ability to rule itself and manage its own affairs. Some feel that membership in international organizations such as the WTO is a threat to their sovereignty.
Compliance	A type of influence process where a receiver accepts the position advocated by a source to obtain favorable outcomes or to avoid punishment is the compliance.
Economy	The income, expenditures, and resources that affect the cost of running a business and household are called an economy.
Analyst	Analyst refers to a person or tool with a primary function of information analysis, generally with a more limited, practical and short term set of goals than a researcher.
Research and development	The use of resources for the deliberate discovery of new information and ways of doing things, together with the application of that information in inventing new products or processes is referred to as research and development.
Economic system	Economic system refers to a particular set of institutional arrangements and a coordinating mechanism for solving the economizing problem; a method of organizing an economy, of which the market system and the command system are the two general types.
United Nations	An international organization created by multilateral treaty in 1945 to promote social and economic cooperation among nations and to protect human rights is the United Nations.
Charter	Charter refers to an instrument or authority from the sovereign power bestowing the right or power to do business under the corporate form of organization. Also, the organic law of a city or town, and representing a portion of the statute law of the state.
Adoption	In corporation law, a corporation's acceptance of a pre-incorporation contract by action of its board of directors, by which the corporation becomes liable on the contract, is referred to as adoption.
Consideration	Consideration in contract law, a basic requirement for an enforceable agreement under traditional contract principles, defined in this text as legal value, bargained for and given in exchange for an act or promise. In corporation law, cash or property contributed to a corporation in exchange for shares, or a promise to contribute such cash or property.
Ad hoc	Ad hoc is a Latin phrase which means "for this purpose." It generally signifies a solution that has been tailored to a specific purpose and is makeshift and non-general, such as a handcrafted network protocol or a specific-purpose equation, as opposed to general solutions.
Committee	A long-lasting, sometimes permanent team in the organization structure created to deal with tasks that recur regularly is the committee.
Task force	A temporary team or committee formed to solve a specific short-term problem involving several departments is the task force.
Verification	Verification refers to the final stage of the creative process where the validity or truthfulness of the insight is determined. The feedback portion of communication in which the receiver sends a message to the source indicating receipt of the message and the degree to which he or she understood the message.
Comprehensive	A comprehensive refers to a layout accurate in size, color, scheme, and other necessary details to show how a final ad will look. For presentation only, never for reproduction.
Accord	An agreement whereby the parties agree to accept something different in satisfaction of the original contract is an accord.

Chapter 9. CONTROLLING THE INSTRUMENTS OF WAR

Chapter 9. CONTROLLING THE INSTRUMENTS OF WAR

Ford	Ford is an American company that manufactures and sells automobiles worldwide. Ford introduced methods for large-scale manufacturing of cars, and large-scale management of an industrial workforce, especially elaborately engineered manufacturing sequences typified by the moving assembly lines.
Administration	Administration refers to the management and direction of the affairs of governments and institutions; a collective term for all policymaking officials of a government; the execution and implementation of public policy.
Restructuring	Restructuring is the corporate management term for the act of partially dismantling and reorganizing a company for the purpose of making it more efficient and therefore more profitable.
Pact	Pact refers to a set of principles endorsed by 21 of the largest U.S. ad agencies aimed at improving the research used in preparing and testing ads, providing a better creative product for clients, and controlling the cost of TV commercials.
Protocol	Protocol refers to a statement that, before product development begins, identifies a well-defined target market; specific customers' needs, wants, and preferences; and what the product will be and do.
Political instability	Events such as riots, revolutions, or government upheavals that affect the operations of an international company is called political instability.
Supply	Supply is the aggregate amount of any material good that can be called into being at a certain price point; it comprises one half of the equation of supply and demand. In classical economic theory, a curve representing supply is one of the factors that produce price.
Control system	A control system is a device or set of devices that manage the behavior of other devices. Some devices or systems are not controllable. A control system is an interconnection of components connected or related in such a manner as to command, direct, or regulate itself or another system.
Scope	Scope of a project is the sum total of all projects products and their requirements or features.
Inventory	Tangible property held for sale in the normal course of business or used in producing goods or services for sale is an inventory.
Decreasing cost	Average cost that declines as output increases, due to increasing returns to scale is called decreasing cost.
Statute	A statute is a formal, written law of a country or state, written and enacted by its legislative authority, perhaps to then be ratified by the highest executive in the government, and finally published.
Technology	The body of knowledge and techniques that can be used to combine economic resources to produce goods and services is called technology.
Export	In economics, an export is any good or commodity, shipped or otherwise transported out of a country, province, town to another part of the world in a legitimate fashion, typically for use in trade or sale.
Economic development	Increase in the economic standard of living of a country's population, normally accomplished by increasing its stocks of physical and human capital and improving its technology is an economic development.
Prohibition	Prohibition refers to denial of the right to import or export, applying to particular products and/or particular countries. Includes embargo.
Dumping	Dumping refers to a practice of charging a very low price in a foreign market for such

Go to **Cram101.com** for the Practice Tests for this Chapter.

Chapter 9. CONTROLLING THE INSTRUMENTS OF WAR

Chapter 9. CONTROLLING THE INSTRUMENTS OF WAR

	economic purposes as putting rival suppliers out of business.
Precedent	A previously decided court decision that is recognized as authority for the disposition of future decisions is a precedent.
Appropriation	A privacy tort that consists of using a person's name or likeness for commercial gain without the person's permission is an appropriation.
Jurisdiction	The power of a court to hear and decide a case is called jurisdiction. It is the practical authority granted to a formally constituted body or to a person to deal with and make pronouncements on legal matters and, by implication, to administer justice within a defined area of responsibility.
Installations	Support goods, consisting of buildings and fixed equipment are called installations.
Acquisition	A company's purchase of the property and obligations of another company is an acquisition.
Association of Southeast Asian Nations	The Association of Southeast Asian Nations is a political, economic, and cultural organization of countries located in Southeast Asia.
Stockpiling	The storage of something in order to have it available in the future if the need for it increases is stockpiling. In international economics, stockpiling occurs for speculative purposes, by governments to provide for national security, and by central banks managing international reserves.
Retaliation	The use of an increased trade barrier in response to another country increasing its trade barrier, either as a way of undoing the adverse effects of the latter's action or of punishing it is retaliation.
Stock	In financial terminology, stock is the capital raized by a corporation, through the issuance and sale of shares.
Intervention	Intervention refers to an activity in which a government buys or sells its currency in the foreign exchange market in order to affect its currency's exchange rate.
Context	The effect of the background under which a message often takes on more and richer meaning is a context. Context is especially important in cross-cultural interactions because some cultures are said to be high context or low context.
International trade	The export of goods and services from a country and the import of goods and services into a country is referred to as the international trade.
Annual report	An annual report is prepared by corporate management that presents financial information including financial statements, footnotes, and the management discussion and analysis.
Coalition	An informal alliance among managers who support a specific goal is called coalition.
Consensus decision making	Consensus decision making is a decision process that not only seeks the agreement of most participants, but also to resolve or mitigate the objections of the minority to achieve the most agreeable decision.
Peak	Peak refers to the point in the business cycle when an economic expansion reaches its highest point before turning down. Contrasts with trough.
Accumulation	The acquisition of an increasing quantity of something. The accumulation of factors, especially capital, is a primary mechanism for economic growth.
Paradox	As used in economics, paradox means something unexpected, rather than the more extreme normal meaning of something seemingly impossible. Some paradoxes are just theoretical results that go against what one thinks of as normal.

Go to **Cram101.com** for the Practice Tests for this Chapter.

Chapter 9. CONTROLLING THE INSTRUMENTS OF WAR

Chapter 9. CONTROLLING THE INSTRUMENTS OF WAR

Possession | Possession refers to respecting real property, exclusive dominion and control such as owners of like property usually exercise over it. Manual control of personal property either as owner or as one having a qualified right in it.

Chapter 9. CONTROLLING THE INSTRUMENTS OF WAR

Chapter 10. VARIETIES OF REGIONALISM

Regionalism	Regionalism refers to the formation or proliferation of preferential trading arrangements within a geographical region.
Security	Security refers to a claim on the borrower future income that is sold by the borrower to the lender. A security is a type of transferable interest representing financial value.
Union	A worker association that bargains with employers over wages and working conditions is called a union.
Appeal	Appeal refers to the act of asking an appellate court to overturn a decision after the trial court's final judgment has been entered.
Scope	Scope of a project is the sum total of all projects products and their requirements or features.
Sovereignty	A country or region's power and ability to rule itself and manage its own affairs. Some feel that membership in international organizations such as the WTO is a threat to their sovereignty.
Integration	Economic integration refers to reducing barriers among countries to transactions and to movements of goods, capital, and labor, including harmonization of laws, regulations, and standards. Integrated markets theoretically function as a unified market.
Market	A market is, as defined in economics, a social arrangement that allows buyers and sellers to discover information and carry out a voluntary exchange of goods or services.
Balance	In banking and accountancy, the outstanding balance is the amount of money owned, (or due), that remains in a deposit account (or a loan account) at a given date, after all past remittances, payments and withdrawal have been accounted for. It can be positive (then, in the balance sheet of a firm, it is an asset) or negative (a liability).
Authority	Authority in agency law, refers to an agent's ability to affect his principal's legal relations with third parties. Also used to refer to an actor's legal power or ability to do something. In addition, sometimes used to refer to a statute, case, or other legal source that justifies a particular result.
Welfare	Welfare refers to the economic well being of an individual, group, or economy. For individuals, it is conceptualized by a utility function. For groups, including countries and the world, it is a tricky philosophical concept, since individuals fare differently.
Aid	Assistance provided by countries and by international institutions such as the World Bank to developing countries in the form of monetary grants, loans at low interest rates, in kind, or a combination of these is called aid. Aid can also refer to assistance of any type rendered to benefit some group or individual.
Accommodation	Accommodation is a term used to describe a delivery of nonconforming goods meant as a partial performance of a contract for the sale of goods, where a full performance is not possible.
Jurisdiction	The power of a court to hear and decide a case is called jurisdiction. It is the practical authority granted to a formally constituted body or to a person to deal with and make pronouncements on legal matters and, by implication, to administer justice within a defined area of responsibility.
Interest	In finance and economics, interest is the price paid by a borrower for the use of a lender's money. In other words, interest is the amount of paid to "rent" money for a period of time.
Promotion	Promotion refers to all the techniques sellers use to motivate people to buy products or services. An attempt by marketers to inform people about products and to persuade them to participate in an exchange.
Misuse	A defense that relieves a seller of product liability if the user abnormally misused the

Chapter 10. VARIETIES OF REGIONALISM

Chapter 10. VARIETIES OF REGIONALISM

	product is called misuse. Products must be designed to protect against foreseeable misuse.
United Nations	An international organization created by multilateral treaty in 1945 to promote social and economic cooperation among nations and to protect human rights is the United Nations.
Charter	Charter refers to an instrument or authority from the sovereign power bestowing the right or power to do business under the corporate form of organization. Also, the organic law of a city or town, and representing a portion of the statute law of the state.
Subsidiary	A company that is controlled by another company or corporation is a subsidiary.
Preponderance	Preponderance of the evidence means that evidence, in the judgment of the juror, is entitled to the greatest weight, appears to be more credible, has greater force, and overcomes not only the opposing presumptions, but also the opposing evidence.
Intervention	Intervention refers to an activity in which a government buys or sells its currency in the foreign exchange market in order to affect its currency's exchange rate.
Preference	The act of a debtor in paying or securing one or more of his creditors in a manner more favorable to them than to other creditors or to the exclusion of such other creditors is a preference. In the absence of statute, a preference is perfectly good, but to be legal it must be bona fide, and not a mere subterfuge of the debtor to secure a future benefit to himself or to prevent the application of his property to his debts.
Channel	Channel, in communications (sometimes called communications channel), refers to the medium used to convey information from a sender (or transmitter) to a receiver.
Consideration	Consideration in contract law, a basic requirement for an enforceable agreement under traditional contract principles, defined in this text as legal value, bargained for and given in exchange for an act or promise. In corporation law, cash or property contributed to a corporation in exchange for shares, or a promise to contribute such cash or property.
Complaint	The pleading in a civil case in which the plaintiff states his claim and requests relief is called complaint. In the common law, it is a formal legal document that sets out the basic facts and legal reasons that the filing party (the plaintiffs) believes are sufficient to support a claim against another person, persons, entity or entities (the defendants) that entitles the plaintiff(s) to a remedy (either money damages or injunctive relief).
Agent	A person who makes economic decisions for another economic actor. A hired manager operates as an agent for a firm's owner.
Economic sanction	A economic sanction can vary from imposing import duties on goods from, or blocking the export of certain goods to the target country, to a full naval blockade of its ports in an effort to verify, and curb or block specified imported goods.
Pact	Pact refers to a set of principles endorsed by 21 of the largest U.S. ad agencies aimed at improving the research used in preparing and testing ads, providing a better creative product for clients, and controlling the cost of TV commercials.
Fragmentation	Fragmentation refers to the splitting of production processes into separate parts that can be done in different locations, including in different countries.
Mediation	Mediation consists of a process of alternative dispute resolution in which a (generally) neutral third party using appropriate techniques, assists two or more parties to help them negotiate an agreement, with concrete effects, on a matter of common interest.
Embargo	Embargo refers to the prohibition of some category of trade. May apply to exports and/or imports, of particular products or of all trade, vis a vis the world or a particular country or countries.
Leadership	Management merely consists of leadership applied to business situations; or in other words:

Chapter 10. VARIETIES OF REGIONALISM

Chapter 10. VARIETIES OF REGIONALISM

	management forms a sub-set of the broader process of leadership.
Economic infrastructure	Economic infrastructure refers to a country's communications, transportation, financial, and distribution systems.
Collaboration	Collaboration occurs when the interaction between groups is very important to goal attainment and the goals are compatible. Wherein people work together —applying both to the work of individuals as well as larger collectives and societies.
Functional organization	Functional organization is a method of organization in which chapters and sections of a manual correspond to business functions, not specific departments or work groups.
Economic union	A common market with the added feature that additional policies -- monetary, fiscal, welfare -- are also harmonized across the member countries is an economic union.
Free trade	Free trade refers to a situation in which there are no artificial barriers to trade, such as tariffs and quotas. Usually used, often only implicitly, with frictionless trade, so that it implies that there are no barriers to trade of any kind.
Customs	Customs is an authority or agency in a country responsible for collecting customs duties and for controlling the flow of people, animals and goods (including personal effects and hazardous items) in and out of the country.
Reorganization	Reorganization occurs, among other instances, when one corporation acquires another in a merger or acquisition, a single corporation divides into two or more entities, or a corporation makes a substantial change in its capital structure.
Restructuring	Restructuring is the corporate management term for the act of partially dismantling and reorganizing a company for the purpose of making it more efficient and therefore more profitable.
Adoption	In corporation law, a corporation's acceptance of a pre-incorporation contract by action of its board of directors, by which the corporation becomes liable on the contract, is referred to as adoption.
Protocol	Protocol refers to a statement that, before product development begins, identifies a well-defined target market; specific customers' needs, wants, and preferences; and what the product will be and do.
Organizational structure	Organizational structure is the way in which the interrelated groups of an organization are constructed. From a managerial point of view the main concerns are ensuring effective communication and coordination.
Committee	A long-lasting, sometimes permanent team in the organization structure created to deal with tasks that recur regularly is the committee.
Sustainable development	Economic development that is achieved without undermining the incomes, resources, or environment of future generations is called sustainable development.
International law	Law that governs affairs between nations and that regulates transactions between individuals and businesses of different countries is an international law.
Comprehensive	A comprehensive refers to a layout accurate in size, color, scheme, and other necessary details to show how a final ad will look. For presentation only, never for reproduction.
Communism	Communism refers to an economic system in which capital is owned by private government. Contrasts with capitalism.
Instrument	Instrument refers to an economic variable that is controlled by policy makers and can be used to influence other variables, called targets. Examples are monetary and fiscal policies used to achieve external and internal balance.

Go to Cram101.com for the Practice Tests for this Chapter.

Chapter 10. VARIETIES OF REGIONALISM

Chapter 10. VARIETIES OF REGIONALISM

Conciliation	A form of mediation in which the parties choose an interested third party to act as the mediator is referred to as conciliation.
Operation	A standardized method or technique that is performed repetitively, often on different materials resulting in different finished goods is called an operation.
Domestic	From or in one's own country. A domestic producer is one that produces inside the home country. A domestic price is the price inside the home country. Opposite of 'foreign' or 'world.'.
Immunity	Granted by law, immunity is the assurance that someone will be exempt from prosecution.
Compatibility	Compatibility refers to used to describe a product characteristic, it means a good fit with other products used by the consumer or with the consumer's lifestyle. Used in a technical context, it means the ability of systems to work together.
Assessment	Collecting information and providing feedback to employees about their behavior, communication style, or skills is an assessment.
Policy	Similar to a script in that a policy can be a less than completely rational decision-making method. Involves the use of a pre-existing set of decision steps for any problem that presents itself.
Mutuality	Reciprocal obligations of the parties required to make a contract binding on either party is referred to as mutuality.
Closing	The finalization of a real estate sales transaction that passes title to the property from the seller to the buyer is referred to as a closing. Closing is a sales term which refers to the process of making a sale. It refers to reaching the final step, which may be an exchange of money or acquiring a signature.
Forming	The first stage of team development, where the team is formed and the objectives for the team are set is referred to as forming.
Common market	Common market refers to a group of countries that eliminate all barriers to movement of both goods and factors among themselves, and that also, on each product, agree to levy the same tariff on imports from outside the group.
Trade association	An industry trade group or trade association is generally a public relations organization founded and funded by corporations that operate in a specific industry. Its purpose is generally to promote that industry through PR activities such as advertizing, education, political donations, political pressure, publishing, and astroturfing.
Cooperative	A business owned and controlled by the people who use it, producers, consumers, or workers with similar needs who pool their resources for mutual gain is called cooperative.
Per capita	Per capita refers to per person. Usually used to indicate the average per person of any given statistic, commonly income.
Economic development	Increase in the economic standard of living of a country's population, normally accomplished by increasing its stocks of physical and human capital and improving its technology is an economic development.
Per capita income	The per capita income for a group of people may be defined as their total personal income, divided by the total population. Per capita income is usually reported in units of currency per year.
Investment	Investment refers to spending for the production and accumulation of capital and additions to inventories. In a financial sense, buying an asset with the expectation of making a return.
Realization	Realization is the sale of assets when an entity is being liquidated.

Chapter 10. VARIETIES OF REGIONALISM

Chapter 10. VARIETIES OF REGIONALISM

Economic growth	Economic growth refers to the increase over time in the capacity of an economy to produce goods and services and to improve the well-being of its citizens.
Developing country	Developing country refers to a country whose per capita income is low by world standards. Same as LDC. As usually used, it does not necessarily connote that the country's income is rising.
Economic policy	Economic policy refers to the actions that governments take in the economic field. It covers the systems for setting interest rates and government deficit as well as the labor market, national ownership, and many other areas of government.
Privatization	A process in which investment bankers take companies that were previously owned by the government to the public markets is referred to as privatization.
Economic forces	Forces that affect the availability, production, and distribution of a society's resources among competing users are referred to as economic forces.
Economy	The income, expenditures, and resources that affect the cost of running a business and household are called an economy.
Free trade area	Free trade area refers to a group of countries that adopt free trade on trade among group members, while not necessarily changing the barriers that each member country has on trade with the countries outside the group.
North American Free Trade Agreement	A 1993 agreement establishing, over a 15-year period, a free trade zone composed of Canada, Mexico, and the United States is referred to as the North American Free Trade Agreement.
Globalization	The increasing world-wide integration of markets for goods, services and capital that attracted special attention in the late 1990s is called globalization.
Applicant	In many tribunal and administrative law suits, the person who initiates the claim is called the applicant.
Condemnation	The process whereby the government acquires the ownership of private property for a public use over the protest of the owner is called condemnation. It is identical to eminent domain.
Negotiation	Negotiation is the process whereby interested parties resolve disputes, agree upon courses of action, bargain for individual or collective advantage, and/or attempt to craft outcomes which serve their mutual interests.
Arbitration	Arbitration is a form of mediation or conciliation, where the mediating party is given power by the disputant parties to settle the dispute by making a finding. In practice arbitration is generally used as a substitute for judicial systems, particularly when the judicial processes are viewed as too slow, expensive or biased. Arbitration is also used by communities which lack formal law, as a substitute for formal law.
Common currency	A situation where several countries form a monetary union with a single currency and a unified central bank is referred to as common currency.
Inception	The date and time on which coverage under an insurance policy takes effect is inception. Also refers to the date at which a stock or mutual fund was first traded.
Ad hoc	Ad hoc is a Latin phrase which means "for this purpose." It generally signifies a solution that has been tailored to a specific purpose and is makeshift and non-general, such as a handcrafted network protocol or a specific-purpose equation, as opposed to general solutions.
Incorporation	Incorporation is the forming of a new corporation. The corporation may be a business, a non-profit organization or even a government of a new city or town.
Verification	Verification refers to the final stage of the creative process where the validity or

Go to Cram101.com for the Practice Tests for this Chapter.

Chapter 10. VARIETIES OF REGIONALISM

Chapter 10. VARIETIES OF REGIONALISM

	truthfulness of the insight is determined. The feedback portion of communication in which the receiver sends a message to the source indicating receipt of the message and the degree to which he or she understood the message.
Disintegration	Disintegration is an organization of production in which different stages of production are divided among different suppliers that are located in different countries.
Management	Management characterizes the process of leading and directing all or part of an organization, often a business, through the deployment and manipulation of resources. Early twentieth-century management writer Mary Parker Follett defined management as "the art of getting things done through people."
Conflict management	Conflict management refers to the long-term management of intractable conflicts. It is the label for the variety of ways by which people handle grievances -- standing up for what they consider to be right and against what they consider to be wrong.
Conflict resolution	Conflict resolution is the process of resolving a dispute or a conflict. Successful conflict resolution occurs by providing each side's needs, and adequately addressing their interests so that they are each satisfied with the outcome. Conflict resolution aims to end conflicts before they start or lead to physical fighting.
Retaliation	The use of an increased trade barrier in response to another country increasing its trade barrier, either as a way of undoing the adverse effects of the latter's action or of punishing it is retaliation.
Treaties	The first source of international law, consisting of agreements or contracts between two or more nations that are formally signed by an authorized representative and ratified by the supreme power of each nation are called treaties.
Pledge	In law a pledge (also pawn) is a bailment of personal property as a security for some debt or engagement.
Dissolution	Dissolution is the process of admitting or removing a partner in a partnership.
Personnel	A collective term for all of the employees of an organization. Personnel is also commonly used to refer to the personnel management function or the organizational unit responsible for administering personnel programs.
Budget	Budget refers to an account, usually for a year, of the planned expenditures and the expected receipts of an entity. For a government, the receipts are tax revenues.
Default	In finance, default occurs when a debtor has not met its legal obligations according to the debt contract, e.g. it has not made a scheduled payment, or violated a covenant (condition) of the debt contract.
Partnership	In the common law, a partnership is a type of business entity in which partners share with each other the profits or losses of the business undertaking in which they have all invested.
Crisis management	Crisis management involves identifying a crisis, planning a response to the crisis and confronting and resolving the crisis.
Economic integration	Occurs when two or more nations join to form a free-trade zone are called economic integration. As economic integration increases, the barriers of trade between markets diminishes.
Tangible	Having a physical existence is referred to as the tangible. Personal property other than real estate, such as cars, boats, stocks, or other assets.
Organizational development	The application of behavioral science knowledge in a longrange effort to improve an organization's ability to cope with change in its external environment and increase its problem-solving capabilities is referred to as organizational development.

Go to Cram101.com for the Practice Tests for this Chapter.

Chapter 10. VARIETIES OF REGIONALISM

Chapter 10. VARIETIES OF REGIONALISM

Customs union	Customs union refers to a group of countries that adopt free trade on trade among themselves, and that also, on each product, agree to levy the same tariff on imports from outside the group. Equivalent to an FTA plus a common external tariff.
Marshall plan	Marshall plan refers to U.S. program to assist the economic recovery of certain European countries after World War II. Also called the European Recovery Program, it was initiated in 1947 and it dispersed over $12 billion before it was completed in 1952.
Recovery	Characterized by rizing output, falling unemployment, rizing profits, and increasing economic activity following a decline is a recovery.
Organization for economic cooperation and development	Organization for economic cooperation and development refers to Paris-based intergovernmental organization of 'wealthy' nations whose purpose is to provide its 29 member states with a forum in which governments can compare their experiences, discuss the problems they share, and seek solutions that can then be applied within their own national contexts.
Annual report	An annual report is prepared by corporate management that presents financial information including financial statements, footnotes, and the management discussion and analysis.
Fund	Independent accounting entity with a self-balancing set of accounts segregated for the purposes of carrying on specific activities is referred to as a fund.
Prerogative	Prerogative refers to a special power, privilege, or immunity, usually used in reference to an official or his office.
Legislative power	Legislative power refers to the power delegated by Congress to an administrative agency to make rules that must be adhered to by individuals and businesses regulated by the agency; these rules have the force of law.
Firm	An organization that employs resources to produce a good or service for profit and owns and operates one or more plants is referred to as a firm.
European Currency Unit	The European Currency Unit was a basket of the currencies of the European Community member states, used as the unit of account of the European Community before being replaced by the euro.
Euro	The common currency of a subset of the countries of the EU, adopted January 1, 1999 is called euro.
Convergence	The blending of various facets of marketing functions and communication technology to create more efficient and expanded synergies is a convergence.
Conversion	Conversion refers to any distinct act of dominion wrongfully exerted over another's personal property in denial of or inconsistent with his rights therein. That tort committed by a person who deals with chattels not belonging to him in a manner that is inconsistent with the ownership of the lawful owner.
Central Bank	Central bank refers to the institution in a country that is normally responsible for managing the supply of the country's money and the value of its currency on the foreign exchange market.
Production	The creation of finished goods and services using the factors of production: land, labor, capital, entrepreneurship, and knowledge.
Incentive	An incentive is any factor (financial or non-financial) that provides a motive for a particular course of action, or counts as a reason for preferring one choice to the alternatives.
Subsidy	Subsidy refers to government financial assistance to a domestic producer.
Labor	People's physical and mental talents and efforts that are used to help produce goods and

Chapter 10. VARIETIES OF REGIONALISM

Chapter 10. VARIETIES OF REGIONALISM

	services are called labor.
Service	Service refers to a "non tangible product" that is not embodied in a physical good and that typically effects some change in another product, person, or institution. Contrasts with good.
Capital	Capital generally refers to financial wealth, especially that used to start or maintain a business. In classical economics, capital is one of four factors of production, the others being land and labor and entrepreneurship.
Capital movement	Capital inflow and/or outflow is referred to as capital movement.
Affiliation	A relationship with other websites in which a company can cross-promote and is credited for sales that accrue through their site is an affiliation.
Tariff	A tax imposed by a nation on an imported good is called a tariff.
Maastricht Treaty	Treaty agreed to in 1991, but not ratified until January 1, 1994, that committed the 12 member states of the European Community to a closer economic and political union is the Maastricht Treaty.
Accession	Accession refers to the process of adding a country to an international agreement, such as the GATT, WTO, EU, or NAFTA.
Administration	Administration refers to the management and direction of the affairs of governments and institutions; a collective term for all policymaking officials of a government; the execution and implementation of public policy.
Market economy	A market economy is an economic system in which the production and distribution of goods and services takes place through the mechanism of free markets guided by a free price system rather than by the state in a planned economy.
Optimum	Optimum refers to the best. Usually refers to a most preferred choice by consumers subject to a budget constraint or a profit maximizing choice by firms or industry subject to a technological constraint.
Industry	A group of firms that produce identical or similar products is an industry. It is also used specifically to refer to an area of economic production focused on manufacturing which involves large amounts of capital investment before any profit can be realized, also called "heavy industry".
Principal	In agency law, one under whose direction an agent acts and for whose benefit that agent acts is a principal.
Stockpiling	The storage of something in order to have it available in the future if the need for it increases is stockpiling. In international economics, stockpiling occurs for speculative purposes, by governments to provide for national security, and by central banks managing international reserves.
Supply	Supply is the aggregate amount of any material good that can be called into being at a certain price point; it comprises one half of the equation of supply and demand. In classical economic theory, a curve representing supply is one of the factors that produce price.
Exchange	The trade of things of value between buyer and seller so that each is better off after the trade is called the exchange.
Exporting	Selling products to another country is called exporting.
Export	In economics, an export is any good or commodity, shipped or otherwise transported out of a country, province, town to another part of the world in a legitimate fashion, typically for use in trade or sale.

Go to Cram101.com for the Practice Tests for this Chapter.

Chapter 10. VARIETIES OF REGIONALISM

Chapter 10. VARIETIES OF REGIONALISM

Boycott	To protest by refusing to purchase from someone, or otherwise do business with them. In international trade, a boycott most often takes the form of refusal to import a country's goods.
Foreign exchange	In finance, foreign exchange means currencies, such as U.S. Dollars and Euros. These are traded on foreign exchange markets.
Accumulation	The acquisition of an increasing quantity of something. The accumulation of factors, especially capital, is a primary mechanism for economic growth.
Petrodollar	Petrodollar refers to the profits made by oil exporting countries when the price rose during the 1970s, and their preference for holding these profits in U.S. dollar-denominated assets, either in the U.S. or in Europe as Eurodollars.
Balance of payments	Balance of payments refers to a list, or accounting, of all of a country's international transactions for a given time period, usually one year.
World price	The price of a good on the 'world market,' meaning the price outside of any country's borders and therefore exclusive of any trade taxes or subsidies is the world price.
Real terms	A wage expressed in real terms is just the real wage.
Recession	A significant decline in economic activity. In the U.S., recession is approximately defined as two successive quarters of falling GDP, as judged by NBER.
Quota	A government-imposed restriction on quantity, or sometimes on total value, used to restrict the import of something to a specific quantity is called a quota.
Financial institution	A financial institution acts as an agent that provides financial services for its clients. Financial institutions generally fall under financial regulation from a government authority.
Allocation of resources	Allocation of resources refers to the society's decisions on how to divide up its scarce input resources among the different outputs produced in the economy, and among the different firms or other organizations that produce those outputs.
Enterprise	Enterprise refers to another name for a business organization. Other similar terms are business firm, sometimes simply business, sometimes simply firm, as well as company, and entity.
Decentralization	Decentralization is the process of redistributing decision-making closer to the point of service or action. This gives freedom to managers at lower levels of the organization to make decisions.
Contribution	In business organization law, the cash or property contributed to a business by its owners is referred to as contribution.
Credit	Credit refers to a recording as positive in the balance of payments, any transaction that gives rise to a payment into the country, such as an export, the sale of an asset, or borrowing from abroad.
Gain	In finance, gain is a profit or an increase in value of an investment such as a stock or bond. Gain is calculated by fair market value or the proceeds from the sale of the investment minus the sum of the purchase price and all costs associated with it.
Regional economic integration	Agreements among countries in a geographic region to reduce and ultimately remove tariff and nontariff barriers to the free flow of goods, services, and factors of production between each other is called regional economic integration.
Expense	In accounting, an expense represents an event in which an asset is used up or a liability is incurred. In terms of the accounting equation, expenses reduce owners' equity.
Trend	Trend refers to the long-term movement of an economic variable, such as its average rate of

Chapter 10. VARIETIES OF REGIONALISM

Chapter 10. VARIETIES OF REGIONALISM

	increase or decrease over enough years to encompass several business cycles.
Transnational	Transnational focuses on the heightened interconnectivity between people all around the world and the loosening of boundaries between countries.

Chapter 10. VARIETIES OF REGIONALISM

Chapter 11. GLOBALIZATION, TRANSNATIONALISM, AND INTERNATIONAL ORGANIZATION

Commodity	Could refer to any good, but in trade a commodity is usually a raw material or primary product that enters into international trade, such as metals or basic agricultural products.
Globalization	The increasing world-wide integration of markets for goods, services and capital that attracted special attention in the late 1990s is called globalization.
Capitalism	Capitalism refers to an economic system in which capital is mostly owned by private individuals and corporations. Contrasts with communism.
Economy	The income, expenditures, and resources that affect the cost of running a business and household are called an economy.
Political economy	Early name for the discipline of economics. A field within economics encompassing several alternatives to neoclassical economics, including Marxist economics. Also called radical political economy.
Prerogative	Prerogative refers to a special power, privilege, or immunity, usually used in reference to an official or his office.
Labor	People's physical and mental talents and efforts that are used to help produce goods and services are called labor.
Sovereignty	A country or region's power and ability to rule itself and manage its own affairs. Some feel that membership in international organizations such as the WTO is a threat to their sovereignty.
Foreign exchange	In finance, foreign exchange means currencies, such as U.S. Dollars and Euros. These are traded on foreign exchange markets.
Exchange	The trade of things of value between buyer and seller so that each is better off after the trade is called the exchange.
Federal Reserve	The Federal Reserve System was created via the Federal Reserve Act of December 23rd, 1913. All national banks were required to join the system and other banks could join. The Reserve Banks opened for business on November 16th, 1914. Federal Reserve Notes were created as part of the legislation, to provide an elastic supply of currency.
Capital flow	International capital movement is referred to as capital flow.
Capital	Capital generally refers to financial wealth, especially that used to start or maintain a business. In classical economics, capital is one of four factors of production, the others being land and labor and entrepreneurship.
Developed country	A developed country is one that enjoys a relatively high standard of living derived through an industrialized, diversified economy. Countries with a very high Human Development Index are generally considered developed countries.
Emerging markets	The term emerging markets is commonly used to describe business and market activity in industrializing or emerging regions of the world. It is sometimes loosely used as a replacement for emerging economies, but really signifies a business phenomenon that is not fully described by or constrained to geography or economic strength; such countries are considered to be in a transitional phase between developing and developed status.
Emerging market	The term emerging market is commonly used to describe business and market activity in industrializing or emerging regions of the world.
Market	A market is, as defined in economics, a social arrangement that allows buyers and sellers to discover information and carry out a voluntary exchange of goods or services.
Service	Service refers to a "non tangible product" that is not embodied in a physical good and that typically effects some change in another product, person, or institution. Contrasts with

Chapter 11. GLOBALIZATION, TRANSNATIONALISM, AND INTERNATIONAL ORGANIZATION

Chapter 11. GLOBALIZATION, TRANSNATIONALISM, AND INTERNATIONAL ORGANIZATION

	good.
Conveyance	A written instrument transferring the title to land or some interest therein from one person to another is the conveyance.
Property	Assets defined in the broadest legal sense. Property includes the unrealized receivables of a cash basis taxpayer, but not services rendered.
Intellectual property	In law, intellectual property is an umbrella term for various legal entitlements which attach to certain types of information, ideas, or other intangibles in their expressed form. The holder of this legal entitlement is generally entitled to exercise various exclusive rights in relation to its subject matter.
Transnational	Transnational focuses on the heightened interconnectivity between people all around the world and the loosening of boundaries between countries.
Interdependence	The extent to which departments depend on each other for resources or materials to accomplish their tasks is referred to as interdependence.
Agent	A person who makes economic decisions for another economic actor. A hired manager operates as an agent for a firm's owner.
United Nations	An international organization created by multilateral treaty in 1945 to promote social and economic cooperation among nations and to protect human rights is the United Nations.
Developing country	Developing country refers to a country whose per capita income is low by world standards. Same as LDC. As usually used, it does not necessarily connote that the country's income is rising.
Channel	Channel, in communications (sometimes called communications channel), refers to the medium used to convey information from a sender (or transmitter) to a receiver.
Corporation	A legal entity chartered by a state or the Federal government that is distinct and separate from the individuals who own it is a corporation. This separation gives the corporation unique powers which other legal entities lack.
Enterprise	Enterprise refers to another name for a business organization. Other similar terms are business firm, sometimes simply business, sometimes simply firm, as well as company, and entity.
Multinational corporation	An organization that manufactures and markets products in many different countries and has multinational stock ownership and multinational management is referred to as multinational corporation.
Trend	Trend refers to the long-term movement of an economic variable, such as its average rate of increase or decrease over enough years to encompass several business cycles.
Transnational corporation	A firm that tries to simultaneously realize gains from experience curve economies, location economies, and global learning, while remaining locally responsive is called transnational corporation.
Interest	In finance and economics, interest is the price paid by a borrower for the use of a lender's money. In other words, interest is the amount of paid to "rent" money for a period of time.
Closing	The finalization of a real estate sales transaction that passes title to the property from the seller to the buyer is referred to as a closing. Closing is a sales term which refers to the process of making a sale. It refers to reaching the final step, which may be an exchange of money or acquiring a signature.
Gap	In December of 1995, Gap became the first major North American retailer to accept independent monitoring of the working conditions in a contract factory producing its garments. Gap is the

Chapter 11. GLOBALIZATION, TRANSNATIONALISM, AND INTERNATIONAL ORGANIZATION

Chapter 11. GLOBALIZATION, TRANSNATIONALISM, AND INTERNATIONAL ORGANIZATION

	largest specialty retailer in the United States.
Conglomerate	A conglomerate is a large company that consists of divisions of often seemingly unrelated businesses.
Multinational corporations	Firms that own production facilities in two or more countries and produce and sell their products globally are referred to as multinational corporations.
Revenue	Revenue is a U.S. business term for the amount of money that a company receives from its activities, mostly from sales of products and/or services to customers.
General Motors	General Motors is the world's largest automaker. Founded in 1908, today it employs about 327,000 people around the world. With global headquarters in Detroit, it manufactures its cars and trucks in 33 countries.
Total revenue	Total revenue refers to the total number of dollars received by a firm from the sale of a product; equal to the total expenditures for the product produced by the firm; equal to the quantity sold multiplied by the price at which it is sold.
Gross National Product	Gross National Product is the total value of final goods and services produced in a year by a country's nationals (including profits from capital held abroad).
Mistake	In contract law a mistake is incorrect understanding by one or more parties to a contract and may be used as grounds to invalidate the agreement. Common law has identified three different types of mistake in contract: unilateral mistake, mutual mistake, and common mistake.
Insurance	Insurance refers to a system by which individuals can reduce their exposure to risk of large losses by spreading the risks among a large number of persons.
Retailing	All activities involved in selling, renting, and providing goods and services to ultimate consumers for personal, family, or household use is referred to as retailing.
Estate	An estate is the totality of the legal rights, interests, entitlements and obligations attaching to property. In the context of wills and probate, it refers to the totality of the property which the deceased owned or in which some interest was held.
Production	The creation of finished goods and services using the factors of production: land, labor, capital, entrepreneurship, and knowledge.
Innovation	Innovation refers to the first commercially successful introduction of a new product, the use of a new method of production, or the creation of a new form of business organization.
Economies of scale	In economics, returns to scale and economies of scale are related terms that describe what happens as the scale of production increases. They are different terms and not to be used interchangeably.
Host country	The country in which the parent-country organization seeks to locate or has already located a facility is a host country.
Technology	The body of knowledge and techniques that can be used to combine economic resources to produce goods and services is called technology.
Personnel	A collective term for all of the employees of an organization. Personnel is also commonly used to refer to the personnel management function or the organizational unit responsible for administering personnel programs.
Bargaining power	Bargaining power refers to the ability to influence the setting of prices or wages, usually arising from some sort of monopoly or monopsony position
Parent company	Parent company refers to the entity that has a controlling influence over another company. It may have its own operations, or it may have been set up solely for the purpose of owning the Subject Company.

Go to **Cram101.com** for the Practice Tests for this Chapter.

Chapter 11. GLOBALIZATION, TRANSNATIONALISM, AND INTERNATIONAL ORGANIZATION

Chapter 11. GLOBALIZATION, TRANSNATIONALISM, AND INTERNATIONAL ORGANIZATION

Firm	An organization that employs resources to produce a good or service for profit and owns and operates one or more plants is referred to as a firm.
Subsidiary	A company that is controlled by another company or corporation is a subsidiary.
Profit	Profit refers to the return to the resource entrepreneurial ability; total revenue minus total cost.
Policy	Similar to a script in that a policy can be a less than completely rational decision-making method. Involves the use of a pre-existing set of decision steps for any problem that presents itself.
Foreign subsidiary	A company owned in a foreign country by another company is referred to as foreign subsidiary.
Management	Management characterizes the process of leading and directing all or part of an organization, often a business, through the deployment and manipulation of resources. Early twentieth-century management writer Mary Parker Follett defined management as "the art of getting things done through people."
Competitive advantage	A business is said to have a competitive advantage when its unique strengths, often based on cost, quality, time, and innovation, offer consumers a greater percieved value and there by differtiating it from its competitors.
Nestle	Nestle is the world's biggest food and beverage company. In the 1860s, a pharmacist, developed a food for babies who were unable to be breastfed. His first success was a premature infant who could not tolerate his own mother's milk nor any of the usual substitutes. The value of the new product was quickly recognized when his new formula saved the child's life.
Union	A worker association that bargains with employers over wages and working conditions is called a union.
Shell	One of the original Seven Sisters, Royal Dutch/Shell is the world's third-largest oil company by revenue, and a major player in the petrochemical industry and the solar energy business. Shell has six core businesses: Exploration and Production, Gas and Power, Downstream, Chemicals, Renewables, and Trading/Shipping, and operates in more than 140 countries.
Nike	Because Nike creates goods for a wide range of sports, they have competition from every sports and sports fashion brand there is. Nike has no direct competitors because there is no single brand which can compete directly with their range of sports and non-sports oriented gear, except for Reebok.
Public relations	Public relations refers to the management function that evaluates public attitudes, changes policies and procedures in response to the public's requests, and executes a program of action and information to earn public understanding and acceptance.
Transparency	Transparency refers to a concept that describes a company being so open to other companies working with it that the once-solid barriers between them become see-through and electronic information is shared as if the companies were one.
Shares	Shares refer to an equity security, representing a shareholder's ownership of a corporation. Shares are one of a finite number of equal portions in the capital of a company, entitling the owner to a proportion of distributed, non-reinvested profits known as dividends and to a portion of the value of the company in case of liquidation.
Investment	Investment refers to spending for the production and accumulation of capital and additions to inventories. In a financial sense, buying an asset with the expectation of making a return.
Wage	The payment for the service of a unit of labor, per unit time. In trade theory, it is the

Go to Cram101.com for the Practice Tests for this Chapter.

Chapter 11. GLOBALIZATION, TRANSNATIONALISM, AND INTERNATIONAL ORGANIZATION

Chapter 11. GLOBALIZATION, TRANSNATIONALISM, AND INTERNATIONAL ORGANIZATION

	only payment to labor, usually unskilled labor. In empirical work, wage data may exclude other compenzation, which must be added to get the total cost of employment.
Income inequality	The unequal distribution of an economy's total income among households or families is called income inequality.
Technological change	The introduction of new methods of production or new products intended to increase the productivity of existing inputs or to raise marginal products is a technological change.
Portfolio	In finance, a portfolio is a collection of investments held by an institution or a private individual. Holding but not always a portfolio is part of an investment and risk-limiting strategy called diversification. By owning several assets, certain types of risk (in particular specific risk) can be reduced.
Portfolio investment	Portfolio investment refers to the acquisition of portfolio capital. Usually refers to such transactions across national borders and/or across currencies.
Operation	A standardized method or technique that is performed repetitively, often on different materials resulting in different finished goods is called an operation.
Direct investment	Direct investment refers to a domestic firm actually investing in and owning a foreign subsidiary or division.
Regulation	Regulation refers to restrictions state and federal laws place on business with regard to the conduct of its activities.
Consumer protection	Consumer protection is government regulation to protect the interests of consumers, for example by requiring businesses to disclose detailed information about products, particularly in areas where safety or public health is an issue, such as food.
Negotiation	Negotiation is the process whereby interested parties resolve disputes, agree upon courses of action, bargain for individual or collective advantage, and/or attempt to craft outcomes which serve their mutual interests.
Patent	The legal right to the proceeds from and control over the use of an invented product or process, granted for a fixed period of time, usually 20 years. Patent is one form of intellectual property that is subject of the TRIPS agreement.
Foreign direct investment	Foreign direct investment refers to the buying of permanent property and businesses in foreign nations.
International management	International management refers to the management of business operations conducted in more than one country.
Economic growth	Economic growth refers to the increase over time in the capacity of an economy to produce goods and services and to improve the well-being of its citizens.
Integration	Economic integration refers to reducing barriers among countries to transactions and to movements of goods, capital, and labor, including harmonization of laws, regulations, and standards. Integrated markets theoretically function as a unified market.
Controlling	A management function that involves determining whether or not an organization is progressing toward its goals and objectives, and taking corrective action if it is not is called controlling.
Multilateral Agreement on Investment	The Multilateral Agreement on Investment was negotiated between members of the Organization for Economic Co-operation and Development (OECD) between 1995 and 1998. Its purpose was to develop multilateral rules that would ensure international invesment was governed in a more systematic and uniform way between states.
Allowance	Reduction in the selling price of goods extended to the buyer because the goods are defective

Go to Cram101.com for the Practice Tests for this Chapter.

Chapter 11. GLOBALIZATION, TRANSNATIONALISM, AND INTERNATIONAL ORGANIZATION

Chapter 11. GLOBALIZATION, TRANSNATIONALISM, AND INTERNATIONAL ORGANIZATION

	or of lower quality than the buyer ordered and to encourage a buyer to keep merchandise that would otherwise be returned is the allowance.
Agenda setting	Agenda setting is the process by which an individual defines the issues to be addressed in the agenda for a meeting, or by which a group of people define the issues to be addressed in a political process.
Subcontractor	A subcontractor is an individual or in many cases a business that signs a contract to perform part or all of the obligations of another's contract. A subcontractor is hired by a general or prime contractor to perform a specific task as part of the overall project.
Authority	Authority in agency law, refers to an agent's ability to affect his principal's legal relations with third parties. Also used to refer to an actor's legal power or ability to do something. In addition, sometimes used to refer to a statute, case, or other legal source that justifies a particular result.
Treaties	The first source of international law, consisting of agreements or contracts between two or more nations that are formally signed by an authorized representative and ratified by the supreme power of each nation are called treaties.
Distribution	Distribution in economics, the manner in which total output and income is distributed among individuals or factors.
International law	Law that governs affairs between nations and that regulates transactions between individuals and businesses of different countries is an international law.
Committee	A long-lasting, sometimes permanent team in the organization structure created to deal with tasks that recur regularly is the committee.
Fund	Independent accounting entity with a self-balancing set of accounts segregated for the purposes of carrying on specific activities is referred to as a fund.
Core	A core is the set of feasible allocations in an economy that cannot be improved upon by subset of the set of the economy's consumers (a coalition). In construction, when the force in an element is within a certain center section, the core, the element will only be under compression.
Sustainable development	Economic development that is achieved without undermining the incomes, resources, or environment of future generations is called sustainable development.
Action plan	Action plan refers to a written document that includes the steps the trainee and manager will take to ensure that training transfers to the job.
Stock	In financial terminology, stock is the capital raized by a corporation, through the issuance and sale of shares.
World Health Organization	The World Health Organization is a specialized agency of the United Nations, acting as a coordinating authority on international public health, headquartered in Geneva, Switzerland. It's constitution states that its mission "is the attainment by all peoples of the highest possible level of health". Its major task is to combat disease, especially key infectious diseases, and to promote the general health of the peoples of the world.
World Bank	The World Bank is a group of five international organizations responsible for providing finance and advice to countries for the purposes of economic development and poverty reduction, and for encouraging and safeguarding international investment.
Staffing	Staffing refers to a management function that includes hiring, motivating, and retaining the best people available to accomplish the company's objectives.
Activism	Activism, in a general sense, can be described as intentional action to bring about social or political change. This action is in support of, or opposition to, one side of an often

Chapter 11. GLOBALIZATION, TRANSNATIONALISM, AND INTERNATIONAL ORGANIZATION

	controversial argument.
Privatization	A process in which investment bankers take companies that were previously owned by the government to the public markets is referred to as privatization.
Bureaucracy	Bureaucracy refers to an organization with many layers of managers who set rules and regulations and oversee all decisions.
Delegation	Delegation is the handing of a task over to another person, usually a subordinate. It is the assignment of authority and responsibility to another person to carry out specific activities.
Charter	Charter refers to an instrument or authority from the sovereign power bestowing the right or power to do business under the corporate form of organization. Also, the organic law of a city or town, and representing a portion of the statute law of the state.
Leadership	Management merely consists of leadership applied to business situations; or in other words: management forms a sub-set of the broader process of leadership.
Endowment	Endowment refers to the amount of something that a person or country simply has, rather than their having somehow to acquire it.
Supply	Supply is the aggregate amount of any material good that can be called into being at a certain price point; it comprises one half of the equation of supply and demand. In classical economic theory, a curve representing supply is one of the factors that produce price.
Tactic	A short-term immediate decision that, in its totality, leads to the achievement of strategic goals is called a tactic.
Condemnation	The process whereby the government acquires the ownership of private property for a public use over the protest of the owner is called condemnation. It is identical to eminent domain.
Context	The effect of the background under which a message often takes on more and richer meaning is a context. Context is especially important in cross-cultural interactions because some cultures are said to be high context or low context.
Scope	Scope of a project is the sum total of all projects products and their requirements or features.
Argument	The discussion by counsel for the respective parties of their contentions on the law and the facts of the case being tried in order to aid the jury in arriving at a correct and just conclusion is called argument.
Administration	Administration refers to the management and direction of the affairs of governments and institutions; a collective term for all policymaking officials of a government; the execution and implementation of public policy.
Civil society	Civil society refers to the name used to encompass a wide and self-selected variety of interest groups, worldwide. It does not include for-profit businesses, government, and government organizations, whereas it does include most non-governmental organizations.
Partnership	In the common law, a partnership is a type of business entity in which partners share with each other the profits or losses of the business undertaking in which they have all invested.
Grant	Grant refers to an intergovernmental transfer of funds . Since the New Deal, state and local governments have become increasingly dependent upon federal grants for an almost infinite variety of programs.
International Atomic Energy Agency	International Atomic Energy Agency was established as an autonomous organization on July 29, 1957. It seeks to promote the peaceful use of nuclear energy and to inhibit its use for military purposes. United States President Dwight D. Eisenhower envisioned, in his "Atoms for

Chapter 11. GLOBALIZATION, TRANSNATIONALISM, AND INTERNATIONAL ORGANIZATION

Chapter 11. GLOBALIZATION, TRANSNATIONALISM, AND INTERNATIONAL ORGANIZATION

	Peace" speech before the UN General Assembly in 1953, the creation of this international body to control and develop the use of atomic energy.
Points	Loan origination fees that may be deductible as interest by a buyer of property. A seller of property who pays points reduces the selling price by the amount of the points paid for the buyer.
Preponderance	Preponderance of the evidence means that evidence, in the judgment of the juror, is entitled to the greatest weight, appears to be more credible, has greater force, and overcomes not only the opposing presumptions, but also the opposing evidence.
Venue	A requirement distinct from jurisdiction that the court be geographically situated so that it is the most appropriate and convenient court to try the case is the venue.
Foundation	A Foundation is a type of philanthropic organization set up by either individuals or institutions as a legal entity (either as a corporation or trust) with the purpose of distributing grants to support causes in line with the goals of the foundation.
Trust	An arrangement in which shareholders of independent firms agree to give up their stock in exchange for trust certificates that entitle them to a share of the trust's common profits.
Restructuring	Restructuring is the corporate management term for the act of partially dismantling and reorganizing a company for the purpose of making it more efficient and therefore more profitable.
Expense	In accounting, an expense represents an event in which an asset is used up or a liability is incurred. In terms of the accounting equation, expenses reduce owners' equity.
Security	Security refers to a claim on the borrower future income that is sold by the borrower to the lender. A security is a type of transferable interest representing financial value.
Yield	The interest rate that equates a future value or an annuity to a given present value is a yield.
Domestic	From or in one's own country. A domestic producer is one that produces inside the home country. A domestic price is the price inside the home country. Opposite of 'foreign' or 'world.'.

Chapter 11. GLOBALIZATION, TRANSNATIONALISM, AND INTERNATIONAL ORGANIZATION

Chapter 12. PROMOTING ECONOMIC WELFARE

United Nations	An international organization created by multilateral treaty in 1945 to promote social and economic cooperation among nations and to protect human rights is the United Nations.
Economic problem	Economic problem refers to how to determine the use of scarce resources among competing uses. Because resources are scarce, the economy must choose what products to produce; how these products are to be produced: and for whom.
World Bank	The World Bank is a group of five international organizations responsible for providing finance and advice to countries for the purposes of economic development and poverty reduction, and for encouraging and safeguarding international investment.
Real value	Real value is the value of anything expressed in money of the day with the effects of inflation removed.
Export	In economics, an export is any good or commodity, shipped or otherwise transported out of a country, province, town to another part of the world in a legitimate fashion, typically for use in trade or sale.
Developing country	Developing country refers to a country whose per capita income is low by world standards. Same as LDC. As usually used, it does not necessarily connote that the country's income is rising.
Production	The creation of finished goods and services using the factors of production: land, labor, capital, entrepreneurship, and knowledge.
Exchange	The trade of things of value between buyer and seller so that each is better off after the trade is called the exchange.
Tariff	A tax imposed by a nation on an imported good is called a tariff.
General Agreement on Tariffs and Trade	The General Agreement on Tariffs and Trade was originally created by the Bretton Woods Conference as part of a larger plan for economic recovery after World War II. It included a reduction in tariffs and other international trade barriers and is generally considered the precursor to the World Trade Organization.
World Trade Organization	The World Trade Organization is an international, multilateral organization, which sets the rules for the global trading system and resolves disputes between its member states, all of whom are signatories to its approximately 30 agreements.
International trade	The export of goods and services from a country and the import of goods and services into a country is referred to as the international trade.
Enterprise	Enterprise refers to another name for a business organization. Other similar terms are business firm, sometimes simply business, sometimes simply firm, as well as company, and entity.
Promotion	Promotion refers to all the techniques sellers use to motivate people to buy products or services. An attempt by marketers to inform people about products and to persuade them to participate in an exchange.
Policy	Similar to a script in that a policy can be a less than completely rational decision-making method. Involves the use of a pre-existing set of decision steps for any problem that presents itself.
Protectionism	Protectionism refers to advocacy of protection. The word has a negative connotation, and few advocates of protection in particular situations will acknowledge being protectionists.
Uruguay round	The eighth and most recent round of trade negotiations under GATT is referred to as Uruguay round.
Negotiation	Negotiation is the process whereby interested parties resolve disputes, agree upon courses of

Go to Cram101.com for the Practice Tests for this Chapter.

Chapter 12. PROMOTING ECONOMIC WELFARE

Chapter 12. PROMOTING ECONOMIC WELFARE

	action, bargain for individual or collective advantage, and/or attempt to craft outcomes which serve their mutual interests.
Trade flow	The quantity or value of a country's bilateral trade with another country is called trade flow.
Trade negotiation	A negotiation between pairs of governments, or among groups of governments, exchanging commitments to alter their trade policies, usually involving reductions in tariffs and sometimes nontariff barriers is a trade negotiation.
Trade barrier	An artificial disincentive to export and/or import, such as a tariff, quota, or other NTB is called a trade barrier.
Subsidy	Subsidy refers to government financial assistance to a domestic producer.
Controlling	A management function that involves determining whether or not an organization is progressing toward its goals and objectives, and taking corrective action if it is not is called controlling.
Preference	The act of a debtor in paying or securing one or more of his creditors in a manner more favorable to them than to other creditors or to the exclusion of such other creditors is a preference. In the absence of statute, a preference is perfectly good, but to be legal it must be bona fide, and not a mere subterfuge of the debtor to secure a future benefit to himself or to prevent the application of his property to his debts.
Commodity	Could refer to any good, but in trade a commodity is usually a raw material or primary product that enters into international trade, such as metals or basic agricultural products.
Exempt	Employees who are not covered by the Fair Labor Standards Act are exempt. Exempt employees are not eligible for overtime pay.
Market	A market is, as defined in economics, a social arrangement that allows buyers and sellers to discover information and carry out a voluntary exchange of goods or services.
Free trade	Free trade refers to a situation in which there are no artificial barriers to trade, such as tariffs and quotas. Usually used, often only implicitly, with frictionless trade, so that it implies that there are no barriers to trade of any kind.
Transparency	Transparency refers to a concept that describes a company being so open to other companies working with it that the once-solid barriers between them become see-through and electronic information is shared as if the companies were one.
Industry	A group of firms that produce identical or similar products is an industry. It is also used specifically to refer to an area of economic production focused on manufacturing which involves large amounts of capital investment before any profit can be realized, also called "heavy industry".
Openness	Openness refers to the extent to which an economy is open, often measured by the ratio of its trade to GDP.
Trade balance	Balance of trade in terms of exports versus imports is called trade balance.
Balance	In banking and accountancy, the outstanding balance is the amount of money owned, (or due), that remains in a deposit account (or a loan account) at a given date, after all past remittances, payments and withdrawal have been accounted for. It can be positive (then, in the balance sheet of a firm, it is an asset) or negative (a liability).
Administration	Administration refers to the management and direction of the affairs of governments and institutions; a collective term for all policymaking officials of a government; the execution and implementation of public policy.

Chapter 12. PROMOTING ECONOMIC WELFARE

Chapter 12. PROMOTING ECONOMIC WELFARE

Domestic	From or in one's own country. A domestic producer is one that produces inside the home country. A domestic price is the price inside the home country. Opposite of 'foreign' or 'world.'.
Applicant	In many tribunal and administrative law suits, the person who initiates the claim is called the applicant.
Budget	Budget refers to an account, usually for a year, of the planned expenditures and the expected receipts of an entity. For a government, the receipts are tax revenues.
Union	A worker association that bargains with employers over wages and working conditions is called a union.
Market price	Market price is an economic concept with commonplace familiarity; it is the price that a good or service is offered at, or will fetch, in the marketplace; it is of interest mainly in the study of microeconomics.
Dumping	Dumping refers to a practice of charging a very low price in a foreign market for such economic purposes as putting rival suppliers out of business.
Welfare	Welfare refers to the economic well being of an individual, group, or economy. For individuals, it is conceptualized by a utility function. For groups, including countries and the world, it is a tricky philosophical concept, since individuals fare differently.
Property	Assets defined in the broadest legal sense. Property includes the unrealized receivables of a cash basis taxpayer, but not services rendered.
Civil society	Civil society refers to the name used to encompass a wide and self-selected variety of interest groups, worldwide. It does not include for-profit businesses, government, and government organizations, whereas it does include most non-governmental organizations.
Interdependence	The extent to which departments depend on each other for resources or materials to accomplish their tasks is referred to as interdependence.
Economic interdependence	Economic interdependence describes countries/nation-states and/or supranational states such as the European Union (EU) or North American Free Trade Agreement (NAFTA) that are interdependent for any (or all) of the following: food, energy, minerals, manufactured goods, multinational/transnational corporations, financial institutions and foreign debt.
Operation	A standardized method or technique that is performed repetitively, often on different materials resulting in different finished goods is called an operation.
Fund	Independent accounting entity with a self-balancing set of accounts segregated for the purposes of carrying on specific activities is referred to as a fund.
International Monetary Fund	The International Monetary Fund is the international organization entrusted with overseeing the global financial system by monitoring exchange rates and balance of payments, as well as offering technical and financial assistance when asked.
Market economy	A market economy is an economic system in which the production and distribution of goods and services takes place through the mechanism of free markets guided by a free price system rather than by the state in a planned economy.
Economy	The income, expenditures, and resources that affect the cost of running a business and household are called an economy.
Dissolution	Dissolution is the process of admitting or removing a partner in a partnership.
Deficit	The deficit is the amount by which expenditure exceed revenue.
Aid	Assistance provided by countries and by international institutions such as the World Bank to developing countries in the form of monetary grants, loans at low interest rates, in kind, or

Chapter 12. PROMOTING ECONOMIC WELFARE

Chapter 12. PROMOTING ECONOMIC WELFARE

	a combination of these is called aid. Aid can also refer to assistance of any type rendered to benefit some group or individual.
Accumulation	The acquisition of an increasing quantity of something. The accumulation of factors, especially capital, is a primary mechanism for economic growth.
Liquidity	Liquidity refers to the capacity to turn assets into cash, or the amount of assets in a portfolio that have that capacity.
Bretton Woods	A 1944 conference in which representatives of 40 countries met to design a new international monetary system is referred to as the Bretton Woods conference.
Bretton Woods system	The Bretton Woods system of international monetary management established the rules for commercial and financial relations among the world's major industrial states. The Bretton Woods system was the first example of a fully-negotiated monetary order intended to govern monetary relations among independent nation-states.
Central Bank	Central bank refers to the institution in a country that is normally responsible for managing the supply of the country's money and the value of its currency on the foreign exchange market.
Management	Management characterizes the process of leading and directing all or part of an organization, often a business, through the deployment and manipulation of resources. Early twentieth-century management writer Mary Parker Follett defined management as "the art of getting things done through people."
Organization for economic cooperation and development	Organization for economic cooperation and development refers to Paris-based intergovernmental organization of 'wealthy' nations whose purpose is to provide its 29 member states with a forum in which governments can compare their experiences, discuss the problems they share, and seek solutions that can then be applied within their own national contexts.
Financial management	The job of managing a firm's resources so it can meet its goals and objectives is called financial management.
Fiscal policy	Fiscal policy refers to any macroeconomic policy involving the levels of government purchases, transfers, or taxes, usually implicitly focused on domestic goods, residents, or firms.
Principal	In agency law, one under whose direction an agent acts and for whose benefit that agent acts is a principal.
Speculation	The purchase or sale of an asset in hopes that its price will rise or fall respectively, in order to make a profit is called speculation.
Exchange rate	Exchange rate refers to the price at which one country's currency trades for another, typically on the exchange market.
Fixed exchange rate	A fixed exchange rate, sometimes is a type of exchange rate regime wherein a currency's value is matched to the value of another single currency or to a basket of other currencies, or to another measure of value, such as gold.
Economic policy	Economic policy refers to the actions that governments take in the economic field. It covers the systems for setting interest rates and government deficit as well as the labor market, national ownership, and many other areas of government.
Gold standard	The gold standard is a monetary system in which the standard economic unit of account is a fixed weight of gold.
Comprehensive	A comprehensive refers to a layout accurate in size, color, scheme, and other necessary details to show how a final ad will look. For presentation only, never for reproduction.

Go to Cram101.com for the Practice Tests for this Chapter.

Chapter 12. PROMOTING ECONOMIC WELFARE

Chapter 12. PROMOTING ECONOMIC WELFARE

Committee	A long-lasting, sometimes permanent team in the organization structure created to deal with tasks that recur regularly is the committee.
International monetary system	International monetary system is a network of international commercial and government institutions that determine currency exchange rates.
Accounting	A system that collects and processes financial information about an organization and reports that information to decision makers is referred to as accounting.
Supply	Supply is the aggregate amount of any material good that can be called into being at a certain price point; it comprises one half of the equation of supply and demand. In classical economic theory, a curve representing supply is one of the factors that produce price.
Special drawing right	Special drawing right refers to what was originally intended within the IMF as a sort of international money for use among central banks pegging their exchange rates. The special drawing right is a transferable right to acquire another country's currency.
Reserve asset	Any asset that is used as international reserves, including a national currency, precious metal such as gold is referred to as a reserve asset.
Basket	A basket is an economic term for a group of several securities created for the purpose of simultaneous buying or selling. Baskets are frequently used for program trading.
Asset	An item of property, such as land, capital, money, a share in ownership, or a claim on others for future payment, such as a bond or a bank deposit is an asset.
Financial market	In economics, a financial market is a mechanism which allows people to trade money for securities or commodities such as gold or other precious metals. In general, any commodity market might be considered to be a financial market, if the usual purpose of traders is not the immediate consumption of the commodity, but rather as a means of delaying or accelerating consumption over time.
Economic development	Increase in the economic standard of living of a country's population, normally accomplished by increasing its stocks of physical and human capital and improving its technology is an economic development.
Common currency	A situation where several countries form a monetary union with a single currency and a unified central bank is referred to as common currency.
Euro	The common currency of a subset of the countries of the EU, adopted January 1, 1999 is called euro.
Monetary policy	The use of the money supply and/or the interest rate to influence the level of economic activity and other policy objectives including the balance of payments or the exchange rate is called monetary policy.
Economics	The social science dealing with the use of scarce resources to obtain the maximum satisfaction of society's virtually unlimited economic wants is an economics.
Foreign exchange	In finance, foreign exchange means currencies, such as U.S. Dollars and Euros. These are traded on foreign exchange markets.
Exchange market	Exchange market refers to the market on which national currencies are bought and sold.
Foreign exchange market	A market for converting the currency of one country into that of another country is called foreign exchange market. It is by far the largest market in the world, in terms of cash value traded, and includes trading between large banks, central banks, currency speculators, multinational corporations, governments, and other financial markets and institutions.
Trade deficit	The amount by which imports exceed exports of goods and services is referred to as trade deficit.

Chapter 12. PROMOTING ECONOMIC WELFARE

Chapter 12. PROMOTING ECONOMIC WELFARE

Depression | Depression refers to a prolonged period characterized by high unemployment, low output and investment, depressed business confidence, falling prices, and widespread business failures. A milder form of business downturn is a recession.

Private bank | A private bank is a bank which is not incorporated, and hence the entirety of its assets are available to meet the liabilities of the bank.

Petrodollar | Petrodollar refers to the profits made by oil exporting countries when the price rose during the 1970s, and their preference for holding these profits in U.S. dollar-denominated assets, either in the U.S. or in Europe as Eurodollars.

Insolvency | Insolvency is a financial condition experienced by a person or business entity when their assets no longer exceed their liabilities or when the person or entity can no longer meet its debt obligations when they come due.

Leadership | Management merely consists of leadership applied to business situations; or in other words: management forms a sub-set of the broader process of leadership.

Default | In finance, default occurs when a debtor has not met its legal obligations according to the debt contract, e.g. it has not made a scheduled payment, or violated a covenant (condition) of the debt contract.

Service charges | Service charges refer to fees charged by a bank for services performed or a penalty for the depositor's failing to maintain a specified minimum cash balance throughout the period.

Service | Service refers to a "non tangible product" that is not embodied in a physical good and that typically effects some change in another product, person, or institution. Contrasts with good.

Economic growth | Economic growth refers to the increase over time in the capacity of an economy to produce goods and services and to improve the well-being of its citizens.

Interest | In finance and economics, interest is the price paid by a borrower for the use of a lender's money. In other words, interest is the amount of paid to "rent" money for a period of time.

Grant | Grant refers to an intergovernmental transfer of funds . Since the New Deal, state and local governments have become increasingly dependent upon federal grants for an almost infinite variety of programs.

Coalition | An informal alliance among managers who support a specific goal is called coalition.

Petition | A petition is a request to an authority, most commonly a government official or public entity. In the colloquial sense, a petition is a document addressed to some official and signed by numerous individuals.

Adoption | In corporation law, a corporation's acceptance of a pre-incorporation contract by action of its board of directors, by which the corporation becomes liable on the contract, is referred to as adoption.

Technology | The body of knowledge and techniques that can be used to combine economic resources to produce goods and services is called technology.

Foundation | A Foundation is a type of philanthropic organization set up by either individuals or institutions as a legal entity (either as a corporation or trust) with the purpose of distributing grants to support causes in line with the goals of the foundation.

Ford | Ford is an American company that manufactures and sells automobiles worldwide. Ford introduced methods for large-scale manufacturing of cars, and large-scale management of an industrial workforce, especially elaborately engineered manufacturing sequences typified by the moving assembly lines.

Chapter 12. PROMOTING ECONOMIC WELFARE

Chapter 12. PROMOTING ECONOMIC WELFARE

Corporation	A legal entity chartered by a state or the Federal government that is distinct and separate from the individuals who own it is a corporation. This separation gives the corporation unique powers which other legal entities lack.
Channel	Channel, in communications (sometimes called communications channel), refers to the medium used to convey information from a sender (or transmitter) to a receiver.
Multinational corporations	Firms that own production facilities in two or more countries and produce and sell their products globally are referred to as multinational corporations.
Multinational corporation	An organization that manufactures and markets products in many different countries and has multinational stock ownership and multinational management is referred to as multinational corporation.
Common market	Common market refers to a group of countries that eliminate all barriers to movement of both goods and factors among themselves, and that also, on each product, agree to levy the same tariff on imports from outside the group.
Assessment	Collecting information and providing feedback to employees about their behavior, communication style, or skills is an assessment.
Investment	Investment refers to spending for the production and accumulation of capital and additions to inventories. In a financial sense, buying an asset with the expectation of making a return.
Profit	Profit refers to the return to the resource entrepreneurial ability; total revenue minus total cost.
Raw material	Raw material refers to a good that has not been transformed by production; a primary product.
Standing	Standing refers to the legal requirement that anyone seeking to challenge a particular action in court must demonstrate that such action substantially affects his legitimate interests before he will be entitled to bring suit.
Ad hoc	Ad hoc is a Latin phrase which means "for this purpose." It generally signifies a solution that has been tailored to a specific purpose and is makeshift and non-general, such as a handcrafted network protocol or a specific-purpose equation, as opposed to general solutions.
Decentralization	Decentralization is the process of redistributing decision-making closer to the point of service or action. This gives freedom to managers at lower levels of the organization to make decisions.
Annual report	An annual report is prepared by corporate management that presents financial information including financial statements, footnotes, and the management discussion and analysis.
Charter	Charter refers to an instrument or authority from the sovereign power bestowing the right or power to do business under the corporate form of organization. Also, the organic law of a city or town, and representing a portion of the statute law of the state.
Consideration	Consideration in contract law, a basic requirement for an enforceable agreement under traditional contract principles, defined in this text as legal value, bargained for and given in exchange for an act or promise. In corporation law, cash or property contributed to a corporation in exchange for shares, or a promise to contribute such cash or property.
Personnel	A collective term for all of the employees of an organization. Personnel is also commonly used to refer to the personnel management function or the organizational unit responsible for administering personnel programs.
Cooperative	A business owned and controlled by the people who use it, producers, consumers, or workers with similar needs who pool their resources for mutual gain is called cooperative.
Affiliation	A relationship with other websites in which a company can cross-promote and is credited for

Chapter 12. PROMOTING ECONOMIC WELFARE

Chapter 12. PROMOTING ECONOMIC WELFARE

	sales that accrue through their site is an affiliation.
Delegation	Delegation is the handing of a task over to another person, usually a subordinate. It is the assignment of authority and responsibility to another person to carry out specific activities.
Precedent	A previously decided court decision that is recognized as authority for the disposition of future decisions is a precedent.
Appreciation	Appreciation refers to a rise in the value of a country's currency on the exchange market, relative either to a particular other currency or to a weighted average of other currencies. The currency is said to appreciate. Opposite of 'depreciation.' Appreciation can also refer to the increase in value of any asset.
Complexity	The technical sophistication of the product and hence the amount of understanding required to use it is referred to as complexity. It is the opposite of simplicity.
Subsidiary	A company that is controlled by another company or corporation is a subsidiary.
Developed country	A developed country is one that enjoys a relatively high standard of living derived through an industrialized, diversified economy. Countries with a very high Human Development Index are generally considered developed countries.
Labor	People's physical and mental talents and efforts that are used to help produce goods and services are called labor.
Revenue	Revenue is a U.S. business term for the amount of money that a company receives from its activities, mostly from sales of products and/or services to customers.
Manufacturing	Production of goods primarily by the application of labor and capital to raw materials and other intermediate inputs, in contrast to agriculture, mining, forestry, fishing, and services a manufacturing.
Manufactured good	A manufactured good refers to goods that have been processed in any way.
Per capita	Per capita refers to per person. Usually used to indicate the average per person of any given statistic, commonly income.
Per capita income	The per capita income for a group of people may be defined as their total personal income, divided by the total population. Per capita income is usually reported in units of currency per year.
Consumption	In Keynesian economics consumption refers to personal consumption expenditure, i.e., the purchase of currently produced goods and services out of income, out of savings (net worth), or from borrowed funds. It refers to that part of disposable income that does not go to saving.
Capital	Capital generally refers to financial wealth, especially that used to start or maintain a business. In classical economics, capital is one of four factors of production, the others being land and labor and entrepreneurship.
Basic skills	Basic skills refer to reading, writing, and communication skills needed to understand the content of a training program.
Productivity	Productivity refers to the total output of goods and services in a given period of time divided by work hours.
Administrator	Administrator refers to the personal representative appointed by a probate court to settle the estate of a deceased person who died.
Incentive	An incentive is any factor (financial or non-financial) that provides a motive for a

Chapter 12. PROMOTING ECONOMIC WELFARE

Chapter 12. PROMOTING ECONOMIC WELFARE

	particular course of action, or counts as a reason for preferring one choice to the alternatives.
Gain	In finance, gain is a profit or an increase in value of an investment such as a stock or bond. Gain is calculated by fair market value or the proceeds from the sale of the investment minus the sum of the purchase price and all costs associated with it.
Diversification	Investing in a collection of assets whose returns do not always move together, with the result that overall risk is lower than for individual assets is referred to as diversification.
Commerce	Commerce is the exchange of something of value between two entities. It is the central mechanism from which capitalism is derived.
Host country	The country in which the parent-country organization seeks to locate or has already located a facility is a host country.
Organizational structure	Organizational structure is the way in which the interrelated groups of an organization are constructed. From a managerial point of view the main concerns are ensuring effective communication and coordination.
Corruption	The unauthorized use of public office for private gain. The most common forms of corruption are bribery, extortion, and the misuse of inside information.
Distribution	Distribution in economics, the manner in which total output and income is distributed among individuals or factors.
Inception	The date and time on which coverage under an insurance policy takes effect is inception. Also refers to the date at which a stock or mutual fund was first traded.
Residual	Residual payments can refer to an ongoing stream of payments in respect of the completion of past achievements.
Allocate	Allocate refers to the assignment of income for various tax purposes. A multistate corporation's nonbusiness income usually is distributed to the state where the nonbusiness assets are located; it is not apportioned with the rest of the entity's income.
Pledge	In law a pledge (also pawn) is a bailment of personal property as a security for some debt or engagement.
Margin	A deposit by a buyer in stocks with a seller or a stockbroker, as security to cover fluctuations in the market in reference to stocks that the buyer has purchased but for which he has not paid is a margin. Commodities are also traded on margin.
Integration	Economic integration refers to reducing barriers among countries to transactions and to movements of goods, capital, and labor, including harmonization of laws, regulations, and standards. Integrated markets theoretically function as a unified market.
Merger	Merger refers to the combination of two firms into a single firm.
Contribution	In business organization law, the cash or property contributed to a business by its owners is referred to as contribution.
Inflation	An increase in the overall price level of an economy, usually as measured by the CPI or by the implicit price deflator is called inflation.
Utility	Utility refers to the want-satisfying power of a good or service; the satisfaction or pleasure a consumer obtains from the consumption of a good or service.
Administrative support	Support services such as personnel, budget, purchasing, data processing which support or facilitate the service programs of the agency are types of administrative support. Also means work assisting an administrator through office management, clerical supervision, data

Go to **Cram101.com** for the Practice Tests for this Chapter.

Chapter 12. PROMOTING ECONOMIC WELFARE

Chapter 12. PROMOTING ECONOMIC WELFARE

	collection and reporting, workflow/project tracking.
Authority	Authority in agency law, refers to an agent's ability to affect his principal's legal relations with third parties. Also used to refer to an actor's legal power or ability to do something. In addition, sometimes used to refer to a statute, case, or other legal source that justifies a particular result.
Instrument	Instrument refers to an economic variable that is controlled by policy makers and can be used to influence other variables, called targets. Examples are monetary and fiscal policies used to achieve external and internal balance.
Fragmentation	Fragmentation refers to the splitting of production processes into separate parts that can be done in different locations, including in different countries.
Concession	A concession is a business operated under a contract or license associated with a degree of exclusivity in exploiting a business within a certain geographical area. For example, sports arenas or public parks may have concession stands; and public services such as water supply may be operated as concessions.
Specificity	The property that a policy measure applies to one or a group of enterprises or industries, as opposed to all industries, is called specificity.
Public sector	Public sector refers to the part of the economy that contains all government entities; government.
Disequilibrium	Inequality or imbalance of supply and demand is referred to as disequilibrium.
Gross domestic product	Gross domestic product refers to the total value of new goods and services produced in a given year within the borders of a country, regardless of by whom.
Real terms	A wage expressed in real terms is just the real wage.
Remainder	A remainder in property law is a future interest created in a transferee that is capable of becoming possessory upon the natural termination of a prior estate created by the same instrument.
Financial institution	A financial institution acts as an agent that provides financial services for its clients. Financial institutions generally fall under financial regulation from a government authority.
Jurisdiction	The power of a court to hear and decide a case is called jurisdiction. It is the practical authority granted to a formally constituted body or to a person to deal with and make pronouncements on legal matters and, by implication, to administer justice within a defined area of responsibility.
Buffer stock	A large quantity of a commodity held in storage to be used to stabilize the commodity's price. This is done by buying when the price is low and adding to the buffer stock, selling out of the buffer stock when the price is high, hoping to reduce the size of price fluctuations.
Stock	In financial terminology, stock is the capital raized by a corporation, through the issuance and sale of shares.
Central planning	The guidance of the economy by direct government control over a large portion of economic activity, as contrasted with allowing markets to serve this purpose is called central planning.
Equity	Equity is the name given to the set of legal principles, in countries following the English common law tradition, which supplement strict rules of law where their application would operate harshly, so as to achieve what is sometimes referred to as "natural justice."
Economic system	Economic system refers to a particular set of institutional arrangements and a coordinating

Chapter 12. PROMOTING ECONOMIC WELFARE

Chapter 12. PROMOTING ECONOMIC WELFARE

	mechanism for solving the economizing problem; a method of organizing an economy, of which the market system and the command system are the two general types.
Gap	In December of 1995, Gap became the first major North American retailer to accept independent monitoring of the working conditions in a contract factory producing its garments. Gap is the largest specialty retailer in the United States.
Sovereignty	A country or region's power and ability to rule itself and manage its own affairs. Some feel that membership in international organizations such as the WTO is a threat to their sovereignty.
Long run	In economic models, the long run time frame assumes no fixed factors of production. Firms can enter or leave the marketplace, and the cost (and availability) of land, labor, raw materials, and capital goods can be assumed to vary.
Closing	The finalization of a real estate sales transaction that passes title to the property from the seller to the buyer is referred to as a closing. Closing is a sales term which refers to the process of making a sale. It refers to reaching the final step, which may be an exchange of money or acquiring a signature.
Mutual interdependence	Mutual interdependence refers to a situation in which a change in price strategy by one firm will affect the sales and profits of another firm. Any firm that makes such a change can expect the other rivals to react to the change. Occurs in oligopolies.
Quota	A government-imposed restriction on quantity, or sometimes on total value, used to restrict the import of something to a specific quantity is called a quota.
Money market	The money market, in macroeconomics and international finance, refers to the equilibration of demand for a country's domestic money to its money supply; market for short-term financial instruments.
Affiliates	Local television stations that are associated with a major network are called affiliates. Affiliates agree to preempt time during specified hours for programming provided by the network and carry the advertising contained in the program.
Partnership	In the common law, a partnership is a type of business entity in which partners share with each other the profits or losses of the business undertaking in which they have all invested.
Holding	The holding is a court's determination of a matter of law based on the issue presented in the particular case. In other words: under this law, with these facts, this result.
Compensatory	Damages that will compensate a part for direct losses due to an injury suffered are referred to as compensatory .
Nonconvertible currency	Nonconvertible currency is currency that both residents and nonresidents are prohibited from converting their holdings of that currency into another currency.
Economic growth rate	The percentage change in the quantity of goods and services produced from one year to the next is referred to as economic growth rate.
Recovery	Characterized by rizing output, falling unemployment, rizing profits, and increasing economic activity following a decline is a recovery.
Beneficiary	The person for whose benefit an insurance policy, trust, will, or contract is established is a beneficiary. In the case of a contract, the beneficiary is called a third-party beneficiary.
Human resources	Human resources refers to the individuals within the firm, and to the portion of the firm's organization that deals with hiring, firing, training, and other personnel issues.
Performance gap	This represents the difference in actual performance shown as compared to the desired

Go to Cram101.com for the Practice Tests for this Chapter.

Chapter 12. PROMOTING ECONOMIC WELFARE

Chapter 12. PROMOTING ECONOMIC WELFARE

	standard of performance. In employee performance management efforts, this performance gap is often described in terms of needed knowledge and skills which become training and development goals for the employee.
Trend	Trend refers to the long-term movement of an economic variable, such as its average rate of increase or decrease over enough years to encompass several business cycles.
Globalization	The increasing world-wide integration of markets for goods, services and capital that attracted special attention in the late 1990s is called globalization.

Chapter 12. PROMOTING ECONOMIC WELFARE

Chapter 13. MANAGING GLOBAL RESOURCES

Industrial revolution	The Industrial Revolution is the stream of new technology and the resulting growth of output that began in England toward the end of the 18th century.
Jurisdiction	The power of a court to hear and decide a case is called jurisdiction. It is the practical authority granted to a formally constituted body or to a person to deal with and make pronouncements on legal matters and, by implication, to administer justice within a defined area of responsibility.
Supply	Supply is the aggregate amount of any material good that can be called into being at a certain price point; it comprises one half of the equation of supply and demand. In classical economic theory, a curve representing supply is one of the factors that produce price.
Management	Management characterizes the process of leading and directing all or part of an organization, often a business, through the deployment and manipulation of resources. Early twentieth-century management writer Mary Parker Follett defined management as "the art of getting things done through people."
Production	The creation of finished goods and services using the factors of production: land, labor, capital, entrepreneurship, and knowledge.
Per capita	Per capita refers to per person. Usually used to indicate the average per person of any given statistic, commonly income.
Union	A worker association that bargains with employers over wages and working conditions is called a union.
Consumption	In Keynesian economics consumption refers to personal consumption expenditure, i.e., the purchase of currently produced goods and services out of income, out of savings (net worth), or from borrowed funds. It refers to that part of disposable income that does not go to saving.
Commodity	Could refer to any good, but in trade a commodity is usually a raw material or primary product that enters into international trade, such as metals or basic agricultural products.
Human resources	Human resources refers to the individuals within the firm, and to the portion of the firm's organization that deals with hiring, firing, training, and other personnel issues.
Economic development	Increase in the economic standard of living of a country's population, normally accomplished by increasing its stocks of physical and human capital and improving its technology is an economic development.
Economic growth	Economic growth refers to the increase over time in the capacity of an economy to produce goods and services and to improve the well-being of its citizens.
Aid	Assistance provided by countries and by international institutions such as the World Bank to developing countries in the form of monetary grants, loans at low interest rates, in kind, or a combination of these is called aid. Aid can also refer to assistance of any type rendered to benefit some group or individual.
United Nations	An international organization created by multilateral treaty in 1945 to promote social and economic cooperation among nations and to protect human rights is the United Nations.
Operation	A standardized method or technique that is performed repetitively, often on different materials resulting in different finished goods is called an operation.
Financial crisis	A loss of confidence in a country's currency or other financial assets causing international investors to withdraw their funds from the country is referred to as a financial crisis.
Personnel	A collective term for all of the employees of an organization. Personnel is also commonly used to refer to the personnel management function or the organizational unit responsible for administering personnel programs.

Go to **Cram101.com** for the Practice Tests for this Chapter.

Chapter 13. MANAGING GLOBAL RESOURCES

Chapter 13. MANAGING GLOBAL RESOURCES

Service	Service refers to a "non tangible product" that is not embodied in a physical good and that typically effects some change in another product, person, or institution. Contrasts with good.
Distribution	Distribution in economics, the manner in which total output and income is distributed among individuals or factors.
Buying power	The dollar amount available to purchase securities on margin is buying power. The amount is calculated by adding the cash held in the brokerage accounts and the amount that could be spent if securities were fully margined to their limit. If an investor uses their buying power, they are purchasing securities on credit.
Welfare	Welfare refers to the economic well being of an individual, group, or economy. For individuals, it is conceptualized by a utility function. For groups, including countries and the world, it is a tricky philosophical concept, since individuals fare differently.
Developing country	Developing country refers to a country whose per capita income is low by world standards. Same as LDC. As usually used, it does not necessarily connote that the country's income is rising.
Affiliates	Local television stations that are associated with a major network are called affiliates. Affiliates agree to preempt time during specified hours for programming provided by the network and carry the advertising contained in the program.
World Bank	The World Bank is a group of five international organizations responsible for providing finance and advice to countries for the purposes of economic development and poverty reduction, and for encouraging and safeguarding international investment.
Fund	Independent accounting entity with a self-balancing set of accounts segregated for the purposes of carrying on specific activities is referred to as a fund.
International Atomic Energy Agency	International Atomic Energy Agency was established as an autonomous organization on July 29, 1957. It seeks to promote the peaceful use of nuclear energy and to inhibit its use for military purposes. United States President Dwight D. Eisenhower envisioned, in his "Atoms for Peace" speech before the UN General Assembly in 1953, the creation of this international body to control and develop the use of atomic energy.
Grant	Grant refers to an intergovernmental transfer of funds . Since the New Deal, state and local governments have become increasingly dependent upon federal grants for an almost infinite variety of programs.
Promotion	Promotion refers to all the techniques sellers use to motivate people to buy products or services. An attempt by marketers to inform people about products and to persuade them to participate in an exchange.
Principal	In agency law, one under whose direction an agent acts and for whose benefit that agent acts is a principal.
Brief	Brief refers to a statement of a party's case or legal arguments, usually prepared by an attorney. Also used to make legal arguments before appellate courts.
Cooperative	A business owned and controlled by the people who use it, producers, consumers, or workers with similar needs who pool their resources for mutual gain is called cooperative.
Trend	Trend refers to the long-term movement of an economic variable, such as its average rate of increase or decrease over enough years to encompass several business cycles.
Enterprise	Enterprise refers to another name for a business organization. Other similar terms are business firm, sometimes simply business, sometimes simply firm, as well as company, and entity.

Go to Cram101.com for the Practice Tests for this Chapter.

Chapter 13. MANAGING GLOBAL RESOURCES

Chapter 13. MANAGING GLOBAL RESOURCES

Contribution	In business organization law, the cash or property contributed to a business by its owners is referred to as contribution.
Policy	Similar to a script in that a policy can be a less than completely rational decision-making method. Involves the use of a pre-existing set of decision steps for any problem that presents itself.
Budget	Budget refers to an account, usually for a year, of the planned expenditures and the expected receipts of an entity. For a government, the receipts are tax revenues.
Administration	Administration refers to the management and direction of the affairs of governments and institutions; a collective term for all policymaking officials of a government; the execution and implementation of public policy.
Committee	A long-lasting, sometimes permanent team in the organization structure created to deal with tasks that recur regularly is the committee.
Wage	The payment for the service of a unit of labor, per unit time. In trade theory, it is the only payment to labor, usually unskilled labor. In empirical work, wage data may exclude other compenzation, which must be added to get the total cost of employment.
Channel	Channel, in communications (sometimes called communications channel), refers to the medium used to convey information from a sender (or transmitter) to a receiver.
Security	Security refers to a claim on the borrower future income that is sold by the borrower to the lender. A security is a type of transferable interest representing financial value.
International Monetary Fund	The International Monetary Fund is the international organization entrusted with overseeing the global financial system by monitoring exchange rates and balance of payments, as well as offering technical and financial assistance when asked.
Investment	Investment refers to spending for the production and accumulation of capital and additions to inventories. In a financial sense, buying an asset with the expectation of making a return.
Capital	Capital generally refers to financial wealth, especially that used to start or maintain a business. In classical economics, capital is one of four factors of production, the others being land and labor and entrepreneurship.
Demographic	A demographic is a term used in marketing and broadcasting, to describe a demographic grouping or a market segment.
Interest	In finance and economics, interest is the price paid by a borrower for the use of a lender's money. In other words, interest is the amount of paid to "rent" money for a period of time.
Assignment	A transfer of property or some right or interest is referred to as assignment.
Specialist	A specialist is a trader who makes a market in one or several stocks and holds the limit order book for those stocks.
Sovereignty	A country or region's power and ability to rule itself and manage its own affairs. Some feel that membership in international organizations such as the WTO is a threat to their sovereignty.
Incentive	An incentive is any factor (financial or non-financial) that provides a motive for a particular course of action, or counts as a reason for preferring one choice to the alternatives.
Adoption	In corporation law, a corporation's acceptance of a pre-incorporation contract by action of its board of directors, by which the corporation becomes liable on the contract, is referred to as adoption.
Economy	The income, expenditures, and resources that affect the cost of running a business and

Chapter 13. MANAGING GLOBAL RESOURCES

Chapter 13. MANAGING GLOBAL RESOURCES

	household are called an economy.
Research and development	The use of resources for the deliberate discovery of new information and ways of doing things, together with the application of that information in inventing new products or processes is referred to as research and development.
Industry	A group of firms that produce identical or similar products is an industry. It is also used specifically to refer to an area of economic production focused on manufacturing which involves large amounts of capital investment before any profit can be realized, also called "heavy industry".
Monopoly	A monopoly is defined as a persistent market situation where there is only one provider of a kind of product or service.
Marketing	Promoting and selling products or services to customers, or prospective customers, is referred to as marketing.
Shell	One of the original Seven Sisters, Royal Dutch/Shell is the world's third-largest oil company by revenue, and a major player in the petrochemical industry and the solar energy business. Shell has six core businesses: Exploration and Production, Gas and Power, Downstream, Chemicals, Renewables, and Trading/Shipping, and operates in more than 140 countries.
British Petroleum	British Petroleum, is a British energy company with headquarters in London, one of four vertically integrated private sector oil, natural gas, and petrol (gasoline) "supermajors" in the world, along with Royal Dutch Shell, ExxonMobil and Total.
Long run	In economic models, the long run time frame assumes no fixed factors of production. Firms can enter or leave the marketplace, and the cost (and availability) of land, labor, raw materials, and capital goods can be assumed to vary.
Cartel	Cartel refers to a group of firms that seeks to raise the price of a good by restricting its supply. The term is usually used for international groups, especially involving state-owned firms and/or governments.
Treaties	The first source of international law, consisting of agreements or contracts between two or more nations that are formally signed by an authorized representative and ratified by the supreme power of each nation are called treaties.
Preparation	Preparation refers to usually the first stage in the creative process. It includes education and formal training.
Consultant	A professional that provides expert advice in a particular field or area in which customers occassionaly require this type of knowledge is a consultant.
Variance	Variance refers to a measure of how much an economic or statistical variable varies across values or observations. Its calculation is the same as that of the covariance, being the covariance of the variable with itself.
Regulation	Regulation refers to restrictions state and federal laws place on business with regard to the conduct of its activities.
Balance	In banking and accountancy, the outstanding balance is the amount of money owned, (or due), that remains in a deposit account (or a loan account) at a given date, after all past remittances, payments and withdrawal have been accounted for. It can be positive (then, in the balance sheet of a firm, it is an asset) or negative (a liability).
Comprehensive	A comprehensive refers to a layout accurate in size, color, scheme, and other necessary details to show how a final ad will look. For presentation only, never for reproduction.
Accumulation	The acquisition of an increasing quantity of something. The accumulation of factors, especially capital, is a primary mechanism for economic growth.

Go to Cram101.com for the Practice Tests for this Chapter.

Chapter 13. MANAGING GLOBAL RESOURCES

Chapter 13. MANAGING GLOBAL RESOURCES

Misuse	A defense that relieves a seller of product liability if the user abnormally misused the product is called misuse. Products must be designed to protect against foreseeable misuse.
World Health Organization	The World Health Organization is a specialized agency of the United Nations, acting as a coordinating authority on international public health, headquartered in Geneva, Switzerland. It's constitution states that its mission "is the attainment by all peoples of the highest possible level of health". Its major task is to combat disease, especially key infectious diseases, and to promote the general health of the peoples of the world.
Toxic substance	Any chemical or mixture whose manufacture, processing, distribution, use, or disposal presents an unreasonable risk of harm to human health or the environment is called toxic substance.
Labor	People's physical and mental talents and efforts that are used to help produce goods and services are called labor.
Host country	The country in which the parent-country organization seeks to locate or has already located a facility is a host country.
Leadership	Management merely consists of leadership applied to business situations; or in other words: management forms a sub-set of the broader process of leadership.
Conciliation	A form of mediation in which the parties choose an interested third party to act as the mediator is referred to as conciliation.
Delegation	Delegation is the handing of a task over to another person, usually a subordinate. It is the assignment of authority and responsibility to another person to carry out specific activities.
Interdependence	The extent to which departments depend on each other for resources or materials to accomplish their tasks is referred to as interdependence.
Action plan	Action plan refers to a written document that includes the steps the trainee and manager will take to ensure that training transfers to the job.
Subsidiary	A company that is controlled by another company or corporation is a subsidiary.
Coercive power	Coercive power refers to the extent to which a person has the ability to punish or physically or psychologically harm someone else.
Transnational	Transnational focuses on the heightened interconnectivity between people all around the world and the loosening of boundaries between countries.
Concession	A concession is a business operated under a contract or license associated with a degree of exclusivity in exploiting a business within a certain geographical area. For example, sports arenas or public parks may have concession stands; and public services such as water supply may be operated as concessions.
Context	The effect of the background under which a message often takes on more and richer meaning is a context. Context is especially important in cross-cultural interactions because some cultures are said to be high context or low context.
Gain	In finance, gain is a profit or an increase in value of an investment such as a stock or bond. Gain is calculated by fair market value or the proceeds from the sale of the investment minus the sum of the purchase price and all costs associated with it.
Technology	The body of knowledge and techniques that can be used to combine economic resources to produce goods and services is called technology.
Recovery	Characterized by rizing output, falling unemployment, rizing profits, and increasing economic activity following a decline is a recovery.

Chapter 13. MANAGING GLOBAL RESOURCES

Chapter 13. MANAGING GLOBAL RESOURCES

Prime minister	The Prime Minister of the United Kingdom of Great Britain and Northern Ireland is the head of government and so exercises many of the executive functions nominally vested in the Sovereign, who is head of state. According to custom, the Prime Minister and the Cabinet (which he or she heads) are accountable for their actions to Parliament, of which they are members by (modern) convention.
Sustainable development	Economic development that is achieved without undermining the incomes, resources, or environment of future generations is called sustainable development.
Reorganization	Reorganization occurs, among other instances, when one corporation acquires another in a merger or acquisition, a single corporation divides into two or more entities, or a corporation makes a substantial change in its capital structure.
Developed country	A developed country is one that enjoys a relatively high standard of living derived through an industrialized, diversified economy. Countries with a very high Human Development Index are generally considered developed countries.
Compromise	Compromise occurs when the interaction is moderately important to meeting goals and the goals are neither completely compatible nor completely incompatible.
Protocol	Protocol refers to a statement that, before product development begins, identifies a well-defined target market; specific customers' needs, wants, and preferences; and what the product will be and do.
National Aeronautics and Space Administration	The National Aeronautics and Space Administration is an agency of the United States Government, responsible for the nation's public space program. Its annual funding amounts to $16 billion and is widely regarded as the forefront leader of space agencies worldwide. In addition to the space program, it is also responsible for long-term civilian and military aerospace research.
Scope	Scope of a project is the sum total of all projects products and their requirements or features.
Authority	Authority in agency law, refers to an agent's ability to affect his principal's legal relations with third parties. Also used to refer to an actor's legal power or ability to do something. In addition, sometimes used to refer to a statute, case, or other legal source that justifies a particular result.
Specie	Specie refers to coins, normally including only those made of precious metal.
Margin	A deposit by a buyer in stocks with a seller or a stockbroker, as security to cover fluctuations in the market in reference to stocks that the buyer has purchased but for which he has not paid is a margin. Commodities are also traded on margin.
Slope	The slope of a line in the plane containing the x and y axes is generally represented by the letter m, and is defined as the change in the y coordinate divided by the corresponding change in the x coordinate, between two distinct points on the line.
Extension	Extension refers to an out-of-court settlement in which creditors agree to allow the firm more time to meet its financial obligations. A new repayment schedule will be developed, subject to the acceptance of creditors.
International law	Law that governs affairs between nations and that regulates transactions between individuals and businesses of different countries is an international law.
Prohibition	Prohibition refers to denial of the right to import or export, applying to particular products and/or particular countries. Includes embargo.
Dumping	Dumping refers to a practice of charging a very low price in a foreign market for such economic purposes as putting rival suppliers out of business.

Chapter 13. MANAGING GLOBAL RESOURCES

Chapter 13. MANAGING GLOBAL RESOURCES

License	A license in the sphere of Intellectual Property Rights (IPR) is a document, contract or agreement giving permission or the 'right' to a legally-definable entity to do something (such as manufacture a product or to use a service), or to apply something (such as a trademark), with the objective of achieving commercial gain.
Privilege	Generally, a legal right to engage in conduct that would otherwise result in legal liability is a privilege. Privileges are commonly classified as absolute or conditional. Occasionally, privilege is also used to denote a legal right to refrain from particular behavior.
Revenue	Revenue is a U.S. business term for the amount of money that a company receives from its activities, mostly from sales of products and/or services to customers.
Objection	In the trial of a case the formal remonstrance made by counsel to something that has been said or done, in order to obtain the court's ruling thereon is an objection.
Negotiation	Negotiation is the process whereby interested parties resolve disputes, agree upon courses of action, bargain for individual or collective advantage, and/or attempt to craft outcomes which serve their mutual interests.
A share	In finance the term A share has two distinct meanings, both relating to securities. The first is a designation for a 'class' of common or preferred stock. A share of common or preferred stock typically has enhanced voting rights or other benefits compared to the other forms of shares that may have been created. The equity structure, or how many types of shares are offered, is determined by the corporate charter.
Depression	Depression refers to a prolonged period characterized by high unemployment, low output and investment, depressed business confidence, falling prices, and widespread business failures. A milder form of business downturn is a recession.

Chapter 13. MANAGING GLOBAL RESOURCES

Chapter 14. PROMOTING SOCIAL PROGRESS

United Nations	An international organization created by multilateral treaty in 1945 to promote social and economic cooperation among nations and to protect human rights is the United Nations.
Charter	Charter refers to an instrument or authority from the sovereign power bestowing the right or power to do business under the corporate form of organization. Also, the organic law of a city or town, and representing a portion of the statute law of the state.
Realization	Realization is the sale of assets when an entity is being liquidated.
Trend	Trend refers to the long-term movement of an economic variable, such as its average rate of increase or decrease over enough years to encompass several business cycles.
Capital	Capital generally refers to financial wealth, especially that used to start or maintain a business. In classical economics, capital is one of four factors of production, the others being land and labor and entrepreneurship.
Developing country	Developing country refers to a country whose per capita income is low by world standards. Same as LDC. As usually used, it does not necessarily connote that the country's income is rising.
Leadership	Management merely consists of leadership applied to business situations; or in other words: management forms a sub-set of the broader process of leadership.
Economic development	Increase in the economic standard of living of a country's population, normally accomplished by increasing its stocks of physical and human capital and improving its technology is an economic development.
Status quo	Status quo is a Latin term meaning the present, current, existing state of affairs.
Tangible	Having a physical existence is referred to as the tangible. Personal property other than real estate, such as cars, boats, stocks, or other assets.
Market	A market is, as defined in economics, a social arrangement that allows buyers and sellers to discover information and carry out a voluntary exchange of goods or services.
Aid	Assistance provided by countries and by international institutions such as the World Bank to developing countries in the form of monetary grants, loans at low interest rates, in kind, or a combination of these is called aid. Aid can also refer to assistance of any type rendered to benefit some group or individual.
Preparation	Preparation refers to usually the first stage in the creative process. It includes education and formal training.
Budget	Budget refers to an account, usually for a year, of the planned expenditures and the expected receipts of an entity. For a government, the receipts are tax revenues.
Sovereignty	A country or region's power and ability to rule itself and manage its own affairs. Some feel that membership in international organizations such as the WTO is a threat to their sovereignty.
Personnel	A collective term for all of the employees of an organization. Personnel is also commonly used to refer to the personnel management function or the organizational unit responsible for administering personnel programs.
Authority	Authority in agency law, refers to an agent's ability to affect his principal's legal relations with third parties. Also used to refer to an actor's legal power or ability to do something. In addition, sometimes used to refer to a statute, case, or other legal source that justifies a particular result.
Channel	Channel, in communications (sometimes called communications channel), refers to the medium used to convey information from a sender (or transmitter) to a receiver.

Chapter 14. PROMOTING SOCIAL PROGRESS

Chapter 14. PROMOTING SOCIAL PROGRESS

Welfare	Welfare refers to the economic well being of an individual, group, or economy. For individuals, it is conceptualized by a utility function. For groups, including countries and the world, it is a tricky philosophical concept, since individuals fare differently.
Escalation	Regarding the structure of tariffs. In the context of a trade war, escalation refers to the increase in tariffs that occurs as countries retaliate again and again.
Cooperative	A business owned and controlled by the people who use it, producers, consumers, or workers with similar needs who pool their resources for mutual gain is called cooperative.
Promotion	Promotion refers to all the techniques sellers use to motivate people to buy products or services. An attempt by marketers to inform people about products and to persuade them to participate in an exchange.
Administrator	Administrator refers to the personal representative appointed by a probate court to settle the estate of a deceased person who died.
Strategic planning	The process of determining the major goals of the organization and the policies and strategies for obtaining and using resources to achieve those goals is called strategic planning.
Regulation	Regulation refers to restrictions state and federal laws place on business with regard to the conduct of its activities.
Scope	Scope of a project is the sum total of all projects products and their requirements or features.
World Health Organization	The World Health Organization is a specialized agency of the United Nations, acting as a coordinating authority on international public health, headquartered in Geneva, Switzerland. It's constitution states that its mission "is the attainment by all peoples of the highest possible level of health". Its major task is to combat disease, especially key infectious diseases, and to promote the general health of the peoples of the world.
Operation	A standardized method or technique that is performed repetitively, often on different materials resulting in different finished goods is called an operation.
Standardization	Standardization, in the context related to technologies and industries, is the process of establishing a technical standard among competing entities in a market, where this will bring benefits without hurting competition.
Sponsorship	When the advertiser assumes responsibility for the production and usually the content of a television program as well as the advertising that appears within it, we have sponsorship.
Principal	In agency law, one under whose direction an agent acts and for whose benefit that agent acts is a principal.
Committee	A long-lasting, sometimes permanent team in the organization structure created to deal with tasks that recur regularly is the committee.
Supply	Supply is the aggregate amount of any material good that can be called into being at a certain price point; it comprises one half of the equation of supply and demand. In classical economic theory, a curve representing supply is one of the factors that produce price.
Exchange	The trade of things of value between buyer and seller so that each is better off after the trade is called the exchange.
Grant	Grant refers to an intergovernmental transfer of funds . Since the New Deal, state and local governments have become increasingly dependent upon federal grants for an almost infinite variety of programs.
Quality control	The measurement of products and services against set standards is referred to as quality

Chapter 14. PROMOTING SOCIAL PROGRESS

	control.
Collaboration	Collaboration occurs when the interaction between groups is very important to goal attainment and the goals are compatible. Wherein people work together —applying both to the work of individuals as well as larger collectives and societies.
Foundation	A Foundation is a type of philanthropic organization set up by either individuals or institutions as a legal entity (either as a corporation or trust) with the purpose of distributing grants to support causes in line with the goals of the foundation.
World Bank	The World Bank is a group of five international organizations responsible for providing finance and advice to countries for the purposes of economic development and poverty reduction, and for encouraging and safeguarding international investment.
Union	A worker association that bargains with employers over wages and working conditions is called a union.
Fund	Independent accounting entity with a self-balancing set of accounts segregated for the purposes of carrying on specific activities is referred to as a fund.
Labor	People's physical and mental talents and efforts that are used to help produce goods and services are called labor.
Restructuring	Restructuring is the corporate management term for the act of partially dismantling and reorganizing a company for the purpose of making it more efficient and therefore more profitable.
Appeal	Appeal refers to the act of asking an appellate court to overturn a decision after the trial court's final judgment has been entered.
Child labor	Originally, the employment of children in a manner detrimental to their health and social development. Now that the law contains strong child labor prohibitions, the term refers to the employment of children below the legal age limit.
Administration	Administration refers to the management and direction of the affairs of governments and institutions; a collective term for all policymaking officials of a government; the execution and implementation of public policy.
Asset	An item of property, such as land, capital, money, a share in ownership, or a claim on others for future payment, such as a bond or a bank deposit is an asset.
Peak	Peak refers to the point in the business cycle when an economic expansion reaches its highest point before turning down. Contrasts with trough.
Contribution	In business organization law, the cash or property contributed to a business by its owners is referred to as contribution.
Assessment	Collecting information and providing feedback to employees about their behavior, communication style, or skills is an assessment.
Multiplier effect	The effect on equilibrium GDP of a change in aggregate expenditures or aggregate demand is called the multiplier effect.
Subsidy	Subsidy refers to government financial assistance to a domestic producer.
Draft	A signed, written order by which one party instructs another party to pay a specified sum to a third party, at sight or at a specific date is a draft.
Instrument	Instrument refers to an economic variable that is controlled by policy makers and can be used to influence other variables, called targets. Examples are monetary and fiscal policies used to achieve external and internal balance.

Go to Cram101.com for the Practice Tests for this Chapter.

Chapter 14. PROMOTING SOCIAL PROGRESS

Chapter 14. PROMOTING SOCIAL PROGRESS

Security	Security refers to a claim on the borrower future income that is sold by the borrower to the lender. A security is a type of transferable interest representing financial value.
Trust	An arrangement in which shareholders of independent firms agree to give up their stock in exchange for trust certificates that entitle them to a share of the trust's common profits.
Corporation	A legal entity chartered by a state or the Federal government that is distinct and separate from the individuals who own it is a corporation. This separation gives the corporation unique powers which other legal entities lack.
Affiliation	A relationship with other websites in which a company can cross-promote and is credited for sales that accrue through their site is an affiliation.
Centralized system	An organizational system whereby advertising along with other marketing activities such as sales, marketing research, and planning are divided along functional lines and are run from one central marketing department is called centralized system.
Organizational structure	Organizational structure is the way in which the interrelated groups of an organization are constructed. From a managerial point of view the main concerns are ensuring effective communication and coordination.
Balance	In banking and accountancy, the outstanding balance is the amount of money owned, (or due), that remains in a deposit account (or a loan account) at a given date, after all past remittances, payments and withdrawal have been accounted for. It can be positive (then, in the balance sheet of a firm, it is an asset) or negative (a liability).
Interest	In finance and economics, interest is the price paid by a borrower for the use of a lender's money. In other words, interest is the amount of paid to "rent" money for a period of time.
Adoption	In corporation law, a corporation's acceptance of a pre-incorporation contract by action of its board of directors, by which the corporation becomes liable on the contract, is referred to as adoption.
Legal system	Legal system refers to system of rules that regulate behavior and the processes by which the laws of a country are enforced and through which redress of grievances is obtained.
Comprehensive	A comprehensive refers to a layout accurate in size, color, scheme, and other necessary details to show how a final ad will look. For presentation only, never for reproduction.
Compliance	A type of influence process where a receiver accepts the position advocated by a source to obtain favorable outcomes or to avoid punishment is the compliance.
Human resources	Human resources refers to the individuals within the firm, and to the portion of the firm's organization that deals with hiring, firing, training, and other personnel issues.
Inter alia	Among other things is called inter alia.
Due process	Due process of law is a legal concept that ensures the government will respect all of a person's legal rights instead of just some or most of those legal rights when the government deprives a person of life, liberty, or property.
Service	Service refers to a "non tangible product" that is not embodied in a physical good and that typically effects some change in another product, person, or institution. Contrasts with good.
Basic skills	Basic skills refer to reading, writing, and communication skills needed to understand the content of a training program.
Inputs	The inputs used by a firm or an economy are the labor, raw materials, electricity and other resources it uses to produce its outputs.
Closing	The finalization of a real estate sales transaction that passes title to the property from

Chapter 14. PROMOTING SOCIAL PROGRESS

Chapter 14. PROMOTING SOCIAL PROGRESS

	the seller to the buyer is referred to as a closing. Closing is a sales term which refers to the process of making a sale. It refers to reaching the final step, which may be an exchange of money or acquiring a signature.
Gap	In December of 1995, Gap became the first major North American retailer to accept independent monitoring of the working conditions in a contract factory producing its garments. Gap is the largest specialty retailer in the United States.
Production	The creation of finished goods and services using the factors of production: land, labor, capital, entrepreneurship, and knowledge.
Information system	An information system is a system whether automated or manual, that comprises people, machines, and/or methods organized to collect, process, transmit, and disseminate data that represent user information.
Cultural values	The values that employees need to have and act on for the organization to act on the strategic values are called cultural values.
Appreciation	Appreciation refers to a rise in the value of a country's currency on the exchange market, relative either to a particular other currency or to a weighted average of other currencies. The currency is said to appreciate. Opposite of 'depreciation.' Appreciation can also refer to the increase in value of any asset.
Diffusion	Diffusion is the process by which a new idea or new product is accepted by the market. The rate of diffusion is the speed that the new idea spreads from one consumer to the next.
Complaint	The pleading in a civil case in which the plaintiff states his claim and requests relief is called complaint. In the common law, it is a formal legal document that sets out the basic facts and legal reasons that the filing party (the plaintiffs) believes are sufficient to support a claim against another person, persons, entity or entities (the defendants) that entitles the plaintiff(s) to a remedy (either money damages or injunctive relief).
Monopoly	A monopoly is defined as a persistent market situation where there is only one provider of a kind of product or service.
Derivative	A derivative is a generic term for specific types of investments from which payoffs over time are derived from the performance of assets (such as commodities, shares or bonds), interest rates, exchange rates, or indices (such as a stock market index, consumer price index (CPI) or an index of weather conditions).
Consumption	In Keynesian economics consumption refers to personal consumption expenditure, i.e., the purchase of currently produced goods and services out of income, out of savings (net worth), or from borrowed funds. It refers to that part of disposable income that does not go to saving.
Export	In economics, an export is any good or commodity, shipped or otherwise transported out of a country, province, town to another part of the world in a legitimate fashion, typically for use in trade or sale.
Stock	In financial terminology, stock is the capital raized by a corporation, through the issuance and sale of shares.
Treaties	The first source of international law, consisting of agreements or contracts between two or more nations that are formally signed by an authorized representative and ratified by the supreme power of each nation are called treaties.
Protocol	Protocol refers to a statement that, before product development begins, identifies a well-defined target market; specific customers' needs, wants, and preferences; and what the product will be and do.

Go to **Cram101.com** for the Practice Tests for this Chapter.

Chapter 14. PROMOTING SOCIAL PROGRESS

Chapter 14. PROMOTING SOCIAL PROGRESS

Complexity	The technical sophistication of the product and hence the amount of understanding required to use it is referred to as complexity. It is the opposite of simplicity.
Pledge	In law a pledge (also pawn) is a bailment of personal property as a security for some debt or engagement.
Cartel	Cartel refers to a group of firms that seeks to raise the price of a good by restricting its supply. The term is usually used for international groups, especially involving state-owned firms and/or governments.
Users	Users refer to people in the organization who actually use the product or service purchased by the buying center.
Regulatory agency	Regulatory agency refers to an agency, commission, or board established by the Federal government or a state government to regulates businesses in the public interest.
Controlling	A management function that involves determining whether or not an organization is progressing toward its goals and objectives, and taking corrective action if it is not is called controlling.
Distribution	Distribution in economics, the manner in which total output and income is distributed among individuals or factors.
Transnational	Transnational focuses on the heightened interconnectivity between people all around the world and the loosening of boundaries between countries.
International dimension	Portion of the external environment that represents events originating in foreign countries as well as opportunities for domestic companies in other countries is called international dimension.
Host country	The country in which the parent-country organization seeks to locate or has already located a facility is a host country.
Conversion	Conversion refers to any distinct act of dominion wrongfully exerted over another's personal property in denial of or inconsistent with his rights therein. That tort committed by a person who deals with chattels not belonging to him in a manner that is inconsistent with the ownership of the lawful owner.
Assimilation	Assimilation refers to the process through which a minority group learns the ways of the dominant group. In organizations, this means that when people of different types and backgrounds are hired, the organization attempts to mold them to fit the existing organizational culture.
Termination	The ending of a corporation that occurs only after the winding-up of the corporation's affairs, the liquidation of its assets, and the distribution of the proceeds to the claimants are referred to as a termination.
Jurisdiction	The power of a court to hear and decide a case is called jurisdiction. It is the practical authority granted to a formally constituted body or to a person to deal with and make pronouncements on legal matters and, by implication, to administer justice within a defined area of responsibility.
Pawn	In law a pledge (also pawn) is a bailment of personal property as a security for some debt or engagement
Accounting	A system that collects and processes financial information about an organization and reports that information to decision makers is referred to as accounting.

Chapter 14. PROMOTING SOCIAL PROGRESS

Chapter 15. HUMAN RIGHTS AND THE STRUGGLE FOR SELF-GOVERNMENT

Contribution	In business organization law, the cash or property contributed to a business by its owners is referred to as contribution.
Promotion	Promotion refers to all the techniques sellers use to motivate people to buy products or services. An attempt by marketers to inform people about products and to persuade them to participate in an exchange.
Welfare	Welfare refers to the economic well being of an individual, group, or economy. For individuals, it is conceptualized by a utility function. For groups, including countries and the world, it is a tricky philosophical concept, since individuals fare differently.
United Nations	An international organization created by multilateral treaty in 1945 to promote social and economic cooperation among nations and to protect human rights is the United Nations.
Interest	In finance and economics, interest is the price paid by a borrower for the use of a lender's money. In other words, interest is the amount of paid to "rent" money for a period of time.
Charter	Charter refers to an instrument or authority from the sovereign power bestowing the right or power to do business under the corporate form of organization. Also, the organic law of a city or town, and representing a portion of the statute law of the state.
Trust	An arrangement in which shareholders of independent firms agree to give up their stock in exchange for trust certificates that entitle them to a share of the trust's common profits.
Peak	Peak refers to the point in the business cycle when an economic expansion reaches its highest point before turning down. Contrasts with trough.
Possession	Possession refers to respecting real property, exclusive dominion and control such as owners of like property usually exercise over it. Manual control of personal property either as owner or as one having a qualified right in it.
Covenant	A covenant is a signed written agreement between two or more parties. Also referred to as a contract.
Annual report	An annual report is prepared by corporate management that presents financial information including financial statements, footnotes, and the management discussion and analysis.
Authority	Authority in agency law, refers to an agent's ability to affect his principal's legal relations with third parties. Also used to refer to an actor's legal power or ability to do something. In addition, sometimes used to refer to a statute, case, or other legal source that justifies a particular result.
Administrator	Administrator refers to the personal representative appointed by a probate court to settle the estate of a deceased person who died.
Right of inspection	A right that shareholders have to inspect the books and records of the corporation is called right of inspection.
Petition	A petition is a request to an authority, most commonly a government official or public entity. In the colloquial sense, a petition is a document addressed to some official and signed by numerous individuals.
Channel	Channel, in communications (sometimes called communications channel), refers to the medium used to convey information from a sender (or transmitter) to a receiver.
Points	Loan origination fees that may be deductible as interest by a buyer of property. A seller of property who pays points reduces the selling price by the amount of the points paid for the buyer.
Administration	Administration refers to the management and direction of the affairs of governments and institutions; a collective term for all policymaking officials of a government; the execution

Go to Cram101.com for the Practice Tests for this Chapter.

Chapter 15. HUMAN RIGHTS AND THE STRUGGLE FOR SELF-GOVERNMENT

Chapter 15. HUMAN RIGHTS AND THE STRUGGLE FOR SELF-GOVERNMENT

	and implementation of public policy.
Sovereignty	A country or region's power and ability to rule itself and manage its own affairs. Some feel that membership in international organizations such as the WTO is a threat to their sovereignty.
Incentive	An incentive is any factor (financial or non-financial) that provides a motive for a particular course of action, or counts as a reason for preferring one choice to the alternatives.
Gain	In finance, gain is a profit or an increase in value of an investment such as a stock or bond. Gain is calculated by fair market value or the proceeds from the sale of the investment minus the sum of the purchase price and all costs associated with it.
Imperialism	Imperialism is a policy of extending control or authority over foreign entities as a means of acquisition and/or maintenance of empires. This is either through direct territorial conquest or settlement, or through indirect methods of exerting control on the politics and/or economy of these other entities. The term is often used to describe the policy of a nation's dominance over distant lands, regardless of whether the nation considers itself part of the empire.
Dissolution	Dissolution is the process of admitting or removing a partner in a partnership.
Entrepreneur	The owner/operator. The person who organizes, manages, and assumes the risks of a firm, taking a new idea or a new product and turning it into a successful business is an entrepreneur.
Enterprise	Enterprise refers to another name for a business organization. Other similar terms are business firm, sometimes simply business, sometimes simply firm, as well as company, and entity.
Management	Management characterizes the process of leading and directing all or part of an organization, often a business, through the deployment and manipulation of resources. Early twentieth-century management writer Mary Parker Follett defined management as "the art of getting things done through people."
Jurisdiction	The power of a court to hear and decide a case is called jurisdiction. It is the practical authority granted to a formally constituted body or to a person to deal with and make pronouncements on legal matters and, by implication, to administer justice within a defined area of responsibility.
Recruitment	Recruitment refers to the set of activities used to obtain a sufficient number of the right people at the right time; its purpose is to select those who best meet the needs of the organization.
Personnel	A collective term for all of the employees of an organization. Personnel is also commonly used to refer to the personnel management function or the organizational unit responsible for administering personnel programs.
Assault	An intentional tort that prohibits any attempt or offer to cause harmful or offensive contact with another if it results in a well-grounded apprehension of imminent battery in the mind of the threatened person is called assault.
Consideration	Consideration in contract law, a basic requirement for an enforceable agreement under traditional contract principles, defined in this text as legal value, bargained for and given in exchange for an act or promise. In corporation law, cash or property contributed to a corporation in exchange for shares, or a promise to contribute such cash or property.
Committee	A long-lasting, sometimes permanent team in the organization structure created to deal with tasks that recur regularly is the committee.

Go to **Cram101.com** for the Practice Tests for this Chapter.

Chapter 15. HUMAN RIGHTS AND THE STRUGGLE FOR SELF-GOVERNMENT

Chapter 15. HUMAN RIGHTS AND THE STRUGGLE FOR SELF-GOVERNMENT

Service	Service refers to a "non tangible product" that is not embodied in a physical good and that typically effects some change in another product, person, or institution. Contrasts with good.
Trustee	An independent party appointed to represent the bondholders is referred to as a trustee.
Assignment	A transfer of property or some right or interest is referred to as assignment.
Operation	A standardized method or technique that is performed repetitively, often on different materials resulting in different finished goods is called an operation.
Security	Security refers to a claim on the borrower future income that is sold by the borrower to the lender. A security is a type of transferable interest representing financial value.
Security interest	A security interest is a property interest created by agreement or by operation of law over assets to secure the performance of an obligation (usually but not always the payment of a debt) which gives the beneficiary of the security interest certain preferential rights in relation to the assets.
Default	In finance, default occurs when a debtor has not met its legal obligations according to the debt contract, e.g. it has not made a scheduled payment, or violated a covenant (condition) of the debt contract.
Closing	The finalization of a real estate sales transaction that passes title to the property from the seller to the buyer is referred to as a closing. Closing is a sales term which refers to the process of making a sale. It refers to reaching the final step, which may be an exchange of money or acquiring a signature.
Privilege	Generally, a legal right to engage in conduct that would otherwise result in legal liability is a privilege. Privileges are commonly classified as absolute or conditional. Occasionally, privilege is also used to denote a legal right to refrain from particular behavior.
Composition	An out-of-court settlement in which creditors agree to accept a fractional settlement on their original claim is referred to as composition.
Adoption	In corporation law, a corporation's acceptance of a pre-incorporation contract by action of its board of directors, by which the corporation becomes liable on the contract, is referred to as adoption.
Union	A worker association that bargains with employers over wages and working conditions is called a union.
Preference	The act of a debtor in paying or securing one or more of his creditors in a manner more favorable to them than to other creditors or to the exclusion of such other creditors is a preference. In the absence of statute, a preference is perfectly good, but to be legal it must be bona fide, and not a mere subterfuge of the debtor to secure a future benefit to himself or to prevent the application of his property to his debts.
Hearing	A hearing is a proceeding before a court or other decision-making body or officer. A hearing is generally distinguished from a trial in that it is usually shorter and often less formal.
Holding	The holding is a court's determination of a matter of law based on the issue presented in the particular case. In other words: under this law, with these facts, this result.
Remainder	A remainder in property law is a future interest created in a transferee that is capable of becoming possessory upon the natural termination of a prior estate created by the same instrument.
Supply	Supply is the aggregate amount of any material good that can be called into being at a certain price point; it comprises one half of the equation of supply and demand. In classical economic theory, a curve representing supply is one of the factors that produce price.

Chapter 15. HUMAN RIGHTS AND THE STRUGGLE FOR SELF-GOVERNMENT

Chapter 15. HUMAN RIGHTS AND THE STRUGGLE FOR SELF-GOVERNMENT

Publicity	Publicity refers to any information about an individual, product, or organization that's distributed to the public through the media and that's not paid for or controlled by the seller.
Compromise	Compromise occurs when the interaction is moderately important to meeting goals and the goals are neither completely compatible nor completely incompatible.
Precedent	A previously decided court decision that is recognized as authority for the disposition of future decisions is a precedent.
Instrument	Instrument refers to an economic variable that is controlled by policy makers and can be used to influence other variables, called targets. Examples are monetary and fiscal policies used to achieve external and internal balance.
Comprehensive	A comprehensive refers to a layout accurate in size, color, scheme, and other necessary details to show how a final ad will look. For presentation only, never for reproduction.
Preparation	Preparation refers to usually the first stage in the creative process. It includes education and formal training.
Termination	The ending of a corporation that occurs only after the winding-up of the corporation's affairs, the liquidation of its assets, and the distribution of the proceeds to the claimants are referred to as a termination.
Emancipation	Emancipation is the act of freeing or being freed/the relinquishment of control; its meaning encompasses both being able to be as one is (or as a political group chooses to be) without having to adjust to another power, while simultaneously being a contributing part or party to the whole.
Residual	Residual payments can refer to an ongoing stream of payments in respect of the completion of past achievements.
Policy	Similar to a script in that a policy can be a less than completely rational decision-making method. Involves the use of a pre-existing set of decision steps for any problem that presents itself.
Economy	The income, expenditures, and resources that affect the cost of running a business and household are called an economy.
Aid	Assistance provided by countries and by international institutions such as the World Bank to developing countries in the form of monetary grants, loans at low interest rates, in kind, or a combination of these is called aid. Aid can also refer to assistance of any type rendered to benefit some group or individual.
Production	The creation of finished goods and services using the factors of production: land, labor, capital, entrepreneurship, and knowledge.
Per capita	Per capita refers to per person. Usually used to indicate the average per person of any given statistic, commonly income.
Concession	A concession is a business operated under a contract or license associated with a degree of exclusivity in exploiting a business within a certain geographical area. For example, sports arenas or public parks may have concession stands; and public services such as water supply may be operated as concessions.
Appeal	Appeal refers to the act of asking an appellate court to overturn a decision after the trial court's final judgment has been entered.
Cooperative	A business owned and controlled by the people who use it, producers, consumers, or workers with similar needs who pool their resources for mutual gain is called cooperative.

Go to Cram101.com for the Practice Tests for this Chapter.

Chapter 15. HUMAN RIGHTS AND THE STRUGGLE FOR SELF-GOVERNMENT

Chapter 15. HUMAN RIGHTS AND THE STRUGGLE FOR SELF-GOVERNMENT

Marxism	The set of social, political, and economic doctrines developed by Karl Marx in the nineteenth century. As an economic theory, Marxism predicted that capitalism would collapse as a result of its own internal contradictions.
Context	The effect of the background under which a message often takes on more and richer meaning is a context. Context is especially important in cross-cultural interactions because some cultures are said to be high context or low context.
Gap	In December of 1995, Gap became the first major North American retailer to accept independent monitoring of the working conditions in a contract factory producing its garments. Gap is the largest specialty retailer in the United States.
Internationa-ization	Internationalization refers to another term for fragmentation. Used by Grossman and Helpman.
Domestic	From or in one's own country. A domestic producer is one that produces inside the home country. A domestic price is the price inside the home country. Opposite of 'foreign' or 'world.'.
Accord	An agreement whereby the parties agree to accept something different in satisfaction of the original contract is an accord.
International law	Law that governs affairs between nations and that regulates transactions between individuals and businesses of different countries is an international law.
Treaties	The first source of international law, consisting of agreements or contracts between two or more nations that are formally signed by an authorized representative and ratified by the supreme power of each nation are called treaties.
Protocol	Protocol refers to a statement that, before product development begins, identifies a well-defined target market; specific customers' needs, wants, and preferences; and what the product will be and do.
Labor	People's physical and mental talents and efforts that are used to help produce goods and services are called labor.
Complaint	The pleading in a civil case in which the plaintiff states his claim and requests relief is called complaint. In the common law, it is a formal legal document that sets out the basic facts and legal reasons that the filing party (the plaintiffs) believes are sufficient to support a claim against another person, persons, entity or entities (the defendants) that entitles the plaintiff(s) to a remedy (either money damages or injunctive relief).
Affirm	To confirm or uphold a former judgment or order of a court is to affirm. Appellate courts, for instance, may affirm the decisions of lower courts.
Compliance	A type of influence process where a receiver accepts the position advocated by a source to obtain favorable outcomes or to avoid punishment is the compliance.
Draft	A signed, written order by which one party instructs another party to pay a specified sum to a third party, at sight or at a specific date is a draft.
Promoter	A person who incorporates a business, organizes its initial management, and raises its initial capital is a promoter.
Testimony	In some contexts, the word bears the same import as the word evidence, but in most connections it has a much narrower meaning. Testimony are the words heard from the witness in court, and evidence is what the jury considers it worth.
Action plan	Action plan refers to a written document that includes the steps the trainee and manager will take to ensure that training transfers to the job.

Chapter 15. HUMAN RIGHTS AND THE STRUGGLE FOR SELF-GOVERNMENT

Chapter 15. HUMAN RIGHTS AND THE STRUGGLE FOR SELF-GOVERNMENT

Developing country	Developing country refers to a country whose per capita income is low by world standards. Same as LDC. As usually used, it does not necessarily connote that the country's income is rising.
Mass media	Mass media refers to non-personal channels of communication that allow a message to be sent to many individuals at one time.
Confirmed	When the seller's bank agrees to assume liability on the letter of credit issued by the buyer's bank the transaction is confirmed. The term means that the credit is not only backed up by the issuing foreign bank, but that payment is also guaranteed by the notifying American bank.
Paradox	As used in economics, paradox means something unexpected, rather than the more extreme normal meaning of something seemingly impossible. Some paradoxes are just theoretical results that go against what one thinks of as normal.
Conciliation	A form of mediation in which the parties choose an interested third party to act as the mediator is referred to as conciliation.
Realization	Realization is the sale of assets when an entity is being liquidated.

Go to **Cram101.com** for the Practice Tests for this Chapter.

Chapter 15. HUMAN RIGHTS AND THE STRUGGLE FOR SELF-GOVERNMENT

Chapter 16. INTERNATIONAL ADMINISTRATION AND THE SEARCH FOR LEADERSHIP

Administration	Administration refers to the management and direction of the affairs of governments and institutions; a collective term for all policymaking officials of a government; the execution and implementation of public policy.
Interest	In finance and economics, interest is the price paid by a borrower for the use of a lender's money. In other words, interest is the amount of paid to "rent" money for a period of time.
Precedent	A previously decided court decision that is recognized as authority for the disposition of future decisions is a precedent.
Civil service	A collective term for all nonmilitary employees of a government. Paramilitary organizations, such as police and firefighters, are always included in civil service counts in the United States. Civil service employment is not the same as merit system employment, because all patronage positions are included in civil service totals.
Service	Service refers to a "non tangible product" that is not embodied in a physical good and that typically effects some change in another product, person, or institution. Contrasts with good.
Administrator	Administrator refers to the personal representative appointed by a probate court to settle the estate of a deceased person who died.
Chancellor	A handful of U.S. states, like Delaware, still maintain a separate Court of Chancery with jurisdiction over equity cases. Judges who sit on those courts is called a chancellor.
Leadership	Management merely consists of leadership applied to business situations; or in other words: management forms a sub-set of the broader process of leadership.
Covenant	A covenant is a signed written agreement between two or more parties. Also referred to as a contract.
Trust	An arrangement in which shareholders of independent firms agree to give up their stock in exchange for trust certificates that entitle them to a share of the trust's common profits.
Labor	People's physical and mental talents and efforts that are used to help produce goods and services are called labor.
Policy	Similar to a script in that a policy can be a less than completely rational decision-making method. Involves the use of a pre-existing set of decision steps for any problem that presents itself.
Functional organization	Functional organization is a method of organization in which chapters and sections of a manual correspond to business functions, not specific departments or work groups.
Composition	An out-of-court settlement in which creditors agree to accept a fractional settlement on their original claim is referred to as composition.
Loyalty	Marketers tend to define customer loyalty as making repeat purchases. Some argue that it should be defined attitudinally as a strongly positive feeling about the brand.
Personnel	A collective term for all of the employees of an organization. Personnel is also commonly used to refer to the personnel management function or the organizational unit responsible for administering personnel programs.
Authority	Authority in agency law, refers to an agent's ability to affect his principal's legal relations with third parties. Also used to refer to an actor's legal power or ability to do something. In addition, sometimes used to refer to a statute, case, or other legal source that justifies a particular result.
Security	Security refers to a claim on the borrower future income that is sold by the borrower to the lender. A security is a type of transferable interest representing financial value.

Chapter 16. INTERNATIONAL ADMINISTRATION AND THE SEARCH FOR LEADERSHIP

Chapter 16. INTERNATIONAL ADMINISTRATION AND THE SEARCH FOR LEADERSHIP

Internationa-ization	Internationalization refers to another term for fragmentation. Used by Grossman and Helpman.
United Nations	An international organization created by multilateral treaty in 1945 to promote social and economic cooperation among nations and to protect human rights is the United Nations.
Distribution	Distribution in economics, the manner in which total output and income is distributed among individuals or factors.
Budget	Budget refers to an account, usually for a year, of the planned expenditures and the expected receipts of an entity. For a government, the receipts are tax revenues.
Holding	The holding is a court's determination of a matter of law based on the issue presented in the particular case. In other words: under this law, with these facts, this result.
Beneficiary	The person for whose benefit an insurance policy, trust, will, or contract is established is a beneficiary. In the case of a contract, the beneficiary is called a third-party beneficiary.
Negotiation	Negotiation is the process whereby interested parties resolve disputes, agree upon courses of action, bargain for individual or collective advantage, and/or attempt to craft outcomes which serve their mutual interests.
Treaties	The first source of international law, consisting of agreements or contracts between two or more nations that are formally signed by an authorized representative and ratified by the supreme power of each nation are called treaties.
Charter	Charter refers to an instrument or authority from the sovereign power bestowing the right or power to do business under the corporate form of organization. Also, the organic law of a city or town, and representing a portion of the statute law of the state.
Recruitment	Recruitment refers to the set of activities used to obtain a sufficient number of the right people at the right time; its purpose is to select those who best meet the needs of the organization.
Quota	A government-imposed restriction on quantity, or sometimes on total value, used to restrict the import of something to a specific quantity is called a quota.
Contribution	In business organization law, the cash or property contributed to a business by its owners is referred to as contribution.
Intrinsic value	Intrinsic value refers to as applied to a warrant, this represents the market value of common stock minus the exercise price. The difference is then multiplied by the number of shares each warrant entitles the holder to purchase.
Compatibility	Compatibility refers to used to describe a product characteristic, it means a good fit with other products used by the consumer or with the consumer's lifestyle. Used in a technical context, it means the ability of systems to work together.
Oath	Any form of attestation by which a person signifies that he is bound in conscience to perform an act faithfully and truthfully is referred to as oath.
Promotion	Promotion refers to all the techniques sellers use to motivate people to buy products or services. An attempt by marketers to inform people about products and to persuade them to participate in an exchange.
Agent	A person who makes economic decisions for another economic actor. A hired manager operates as an agent for a firm's owner.
Attachment	Attachment in general, the process of taking a person's property under an appropriate judicial order by an appropriate officer of the court. Used for a variety of purposes,

Go to Cram101.com for the Practice Tests for this Chapter.

Chapter 16. INTERNATIONAL ADMINISTRATION AND THE SEARCH FOR LEADERSHIP

Chapter 16. INTERNATIONAL ADMINISTRATION AND THE SEARCH FOR LEADERSHIP

	including the acquisition of jurisdiction over the property seized and the securing of property that may be used to satisfy a debt.
Cooperative	A business owned and controlled by the people who use it, producers, consumers, or workers with similar needs who pool their resources for mutual gain is called cooperative.
Enterprise	Enterprise refers to another name for a business organization. Other similar terms are business firm, sometimes simply business, sometimes simply firm, as well as company, and entity.
Assignment	A transfer of property or some right or interest is referred to as assignment.
Contract	A contract is a "promise" or an "agreement" that is enforced or recognized by the law. In the civil law, a contract is considered to be part of the general law of obligations.
Affiliation	A relationship with other websites in which a company can cross-promote and is credited for sales that accrue through their site is an affiliation.
Allegation	An allegation is a statement of a fact by a party in a pleading, which the party claims it will prove. Allegations remain assertions without proof, only claims until they are proved.
Grand jury	A grand jury is a type of common law jury responsible for investigating alleged crimes, examining evidence, and issuing indictments if they believe that there is enough evidence for a trial to proceed. A grand jury is distinguished from a petit jury, which is used during trial; the names refer to their respective sizes (typically 25 and 12 members respectively).
Jury	A body of lay persons, selected by lot, or by some other fair and impartial means, to ascertain, under the guidance of the judge, the truth in questions of fact arising either in civil litigation or a criminal process is referred to as jury.
Judiciary	The branch of government chosen to oversee the legal system through the court system is referred to as judiciary.
Committee	A long-lasting, sometimes permanent team in the organization structure created to deal with tasks that recur regularly is the committee.
Hearing	A hearing is a proceeding before a court or other decision-making body or officer. A hearing is generally distinguished from a trial in that it is usually shorter and often less formal.
Jurisdiction	The power of a court to hear and decide a case is called jurisdiction. It is the practical authority granted to a formally constituted body or to a person to deal with and make pronouncements on legal matters and, by implication, to administer justice within a defined area of responsibility.
Host country	The country in which the parent-country organization seeks to locate or has already located a facility is a host country.
Appeal	Appeal refers to the act of asking an appellate court to overturn a decision after the trial court's final judgment has been entered.
Regulation	Regulation refers to restrictions state and federal laws place on business with regard to the conduct of its activities.
Executive order	A legal rule issued by a chief executive usually pursuant to a delegation of power from the legislature is called executive order.
Recovery	Characterized by rizing output, falling unemployment, rizing profits, and increasing economic activity following a decline is a recovery.
Applicant	In many tribunal and administrative law suits, the person who initiates the claim is called the applicant.

Go to **Cram101.com** for the Practice Tests for this Chapter.

Chapter 16. INTERNATIONAL ADMINISTRATION AND THE SEARCH FOR LEADERSHIP

Chapter 16. INTERNATIONAL ADMINISTRATION AND THE SEARCH FOR LEADERSHIP

Preference	The act of a debtor in paying or securing one or more of his creditors in a manner more favorable to them than to other creditors or to the exclusion of such other creditors is a preference. In the absence of statute, a preference is perfectly good, but to be legal it must be bona fide, and not a mere subterfuge of the debtor to secure a future benefit to himself or to prevent the application of his property to his debts.
Balance	In banking and accountancy, the outstanding balance is the amount of money owned, (or due), that remains in a deposit account (or a loan account) at a given date, after all past remittances, payments and withdrawal have been accounted for. It can be positive (then, in the balance sheet of a firm, it is an asset) or negative (a liability).
Privilege	Generally, a legal right to engage in conduct that would otherwise result in legal liability is a privilege. Privileges are commonly classified as absolute or conditional. Occasionally, privilege is also used to denote a legal right to refrain from particular behavior.
Immunity	Granted by law, immunity is the assurance that someone will be exempt from prosecution.
Accord	An agreement whereby the parties agree to accept something different in satisfaction of the original contract is an accord.
Assessment	Collecting information and providing feedback to employees about their behavior, communication style, or skills is an assessment.
Management	Management characterizes the process of leading and directing all or part of an organization, often a business, through the deployment and manipulation of resources. Early twentieth-century management writer Mary Parker Follett defined management as "the art of getting things done through people."
Complexity	The technical sophistication of the product and hence the amount of understanding required to use it is referred to as complexity. It is the opposite of simplicity.
Corporation	A legal entity chartered by a state or the Federal government that is distinct and separate from the individuals who own it is a corporation. This separation gives the corporation unique powers which other legal entities lack.
Operation	A standardized method or technique that is performed repetitively, often on different materials resulting in different finished goods is called an operation.
Cultural values	The values that employees need to have and act on for the organization to act on the strategic values are called cultural values.
Specialist	A specialist is a trader who makes a market in one or several stocks and holds the limit order book for those stocks.
Exempt	Employees who are not covered by the Fair Labor Standards Act are exempt. Exempt employees are not eligible for overtime pay.
Market	A market is, as defined in economics, a social arrangement that allows buyers and sellers to discover information and carry out a voluntary exchange of goods or services.
Expense	In accounting, an expense represents an event in which an asset is used up or a liability is incurred. In terms of the accounting equation, expenses reduce owners' equity.
Fund	Independent accounting entity with a self-balancing set of accounts segregated for the purposes of carrying on specific activities is referred to as a fund.
Plea	A plea is an answer to a declaration or complaint or any material allegation of fact therein that, if untrue, would defeat the action. In criminal procedure, a plea is the matter that the accused, on his arraignment, alleges in answer to the charge against him.
Bankruptcy	Bankruptcy is a legally declared inability or impairment of ability of an individual or

Go to **Cram101.com** for the Practice Tests for this Chapter.

Chapter 16. INTERNATIONAL ADMINISTRATION AND THE SEARCH FOR LEADERSHIP

Chapter 16. INTERNATIONAL ADMINISTRATION AND THE SEARCH FOR LEADERSHIP

	organization to pay their creditors.
Delegation	Delegation is the handing of a task over to another person, usually a subordinate. It is the assignment of authority and responsibility to another person to carry out specific activities.
Jargon	Jargon is terminology, much like slang, that relates to a specific activity, profession, or group. It develops as a kind of shorthand, to express ideas that are frequently discussed between members of a group, and can also have the effect of distinguishing those belonging to a group from those who are not.
Aid	Assistance provided by countries and by international institutions such as the World Bank to developing countries in the form of monetary grants, loans at low interest rates, in kind, or a combination of these is called aid. Aid can also refer to assistance of any type rendered to benefit some group or individual.
Teamwork	That which occurs when group members work together in ways that utilize their skills well to accomplish a purpose is called teamwork.
Annual report	An annual report is prepared by corporate management that presents financial information including financial statements, footnotes, and the management discussion and analysis.
Activism	Activism, in a general sense, can be described as intentional action to bring about social or political change. This action is in support of, or opposition to, one side of an often controversial argument.
Grant	Grant refers to an intergovernmental transfer of funds . Since the New Deal, state and local governments have become increasingly dependent upon federal grants for an almost infinite variety of programs.
Instrument	Instrument refers to an economic variable that is controlled by policy makers and can be used to influence other variables, called targets. Examples are monetary and fiscal policies used to achieve external and internal balance.
Union	A worker association that bargains with employers over wages and working conditions is called a union.
Portfolio	In finance, a portfolio is a collection of investments held by an institution or a private individual. Holding but not always a portfolio is part of an investment and risk-limiting strategy called diversification. By owning several assets, certain types of risk (in particular specific risk) can be reduced.
Immobility	The inability or unwillingness of a worker to move from one geographic area or occupation to another or from a lower-paying job to a higher-paying job is immobility.
Innovation	Innovation refers to the first commercially successful introduction of a new product, the use of a new method of production, or the creation of a new form of business organization.
Welfare	Welfare refers to the economic well being of an individual, group, or economy. For individuals, it is conceptualized by a utility function. For groups, including countries and the world, it is a tricky philosophical concept, since individuals fare differently.
Economy	The income, expenditures, and resources that affect the cost of running a business and household are called an economy.
Extension	Extension refers to an out-of-court settlement in which creditors agree to allow the firm more time to meet its financial obligations. A new repayment schedule will be developed, subject to the acceptance of creditors.
Prerogative	Prerogative refers to a special power, privilege, or immunity, usually used in reference to an official or his office.

Go to **Cram101.com** for the Practice Tests for this Chapter.

Chapter 16. INTERNATIONAL ADMINISTRATION AND THE SEARCH FOR LEADERSHIP

Chapter 16. INTERNATIONAL ADMINISTRATION AND THE SEARCH FOR LEADERSHIP

Partition	Partition refers to proceeding the object of which is to enable those who own property as joint tenants or tenants in common to put an end to the tenancy so as to vest in each a sole estate in specific property or an allotment of the lands and tenements. If a division of the estate is impracticable, the estate ought to be sold and the proceeds divided.
Remainder	A remainder in property law is a future interest created in a transferee that is capable of becoming possessory upon the natural termination of a prior estate created by the same instrument.
Sovereignty	A country or region's power and ability to rule itself and manage its own affairs. Some feel that membership in international organizations such as the WTO is a threat to their sovereignty.
Compliance	A type of influence process where a receiver accepts the position advocated by a source to obtain favorable outcomes or to avoid punishment is the compliance.
Adoption	In corporation law, a corporation's acceptance of a pre-incorporation contract by action of its board of directors, by which the corporation becomes liable on the contract, is referred to as adoption.
Intervention	Intervention refers to an activity in which a government buys or sells its currency in the foreign exchange market in order to affect its currency's exchange rate.
Specificity	The property that a policy measure applies to one or a group of enterprises or industries, as opposed to all industries, is called specificity.
Pledge	In law a pledge (also pawn) is a bailment of personal property as a security for some debt or engagement.
Peak	Peak refers to the point in the business cycle when an economic expansion reaches its highest point before turning down. Contrasts with trough.
Controlling	A management function that involves determining whether or not an organization is progressing toward its goals and objectives, and taking corrective action if it is not is called controlling.
Mediation	Mediation consists of a process of alternative dispute resolution in which a (generally) neutral third party using appropriate techniques, assists two or more parties to help them negotiate an agreement, with concrete effects, on a matter of common interest.
Crisis management	Crisis management involves identifying a crisis, planning a response to the crisis and confronting and resolving the crisis.
Trend	Trend refers to the long-term movement of an economic variable, such as its average rate of increase or decrease over enough years to encompass several business cycles.
Conflict resolution	Conflict resolution is the process of resolving a dispute or a conflict. Successful conflict resolution occurs by providing each side's needs, and adequately addressing their interests so that they are each satisfied with the outcome. Conflict resolution aims to end conflicts before they start or lead to physical fighting.
Bureaucracy	Bureaucracy refers to an organization with many layers of managers who set rules and regulations and oversee all decisions.
Inflation	An increase in the overall price level of an economy, usually as measured by the CPI or by the implicit price deflator is called inflation.
Credit	Credit refers to a recording as positive in the balance of payments, any transaction that gives rise to a payment into the country, such as an export, the sale of an asset, or borrowing from abroad.

Go to **Cram101.com** for the Practice Tests for this Chapter.

Chapter 16. INTERNATIONAL ADMINISTRATION AND THE SEARCH FOR LEADERSHIP

Chapter 16. INTERNATIONAL ADMINISTRATION AND THE SEARCH FOR LEADERSHIP

Firm	An organization that employs resources to produce a good or service for profit and owns and operates one or more plants is referred to as a firm.
Optimum	Optimum refers to the best. Usually refers to a most preferred choice by consumers subject to a budget constraint or a profit maximizing choice by firms or industry subject to a technological constraint.
Foundation	A Foundation is a type of philanthropic organization set up by either individuals or institutions as a legal entity (either as a corporation or trust) with the purpose of distributing grants to support causes in line with the goals of the foundation.
Ford	Ford is an American company that manufactures and sells automobiles worldwide. Ford introduced methods for large-scale manufacturing of cars, and large-scale management of an industrial workforce, especially elaborately engineered manufacturing sequences typified by the moving assembly lines.
Staffing	Staffing refers to a management function that includes hiring, motivating, and retaining the best people available to accomplish the company's objectives.
Channel	Channel, in communications (sometimes called communications channel), refers to the medium used to convey information from a sender (or transmitter) to a receiver.

Chapter 16. INTERNATIONAL ADMINISTRATION AND THE SEARCH FOR LEADERSHIP

Chapter 17. INTERNATIONAL ORGANIZATION IN RETROSPECT AND PROSPECT

Assessment	Collecting information and providing feedback to employees about their behavior, communication style, or skills is an assessment.
Contribution	In business organization law, the cash or property contributed to a business by its owners is referred to as contribution.
Aid	Assistance provided by countries and by international institutions such as the World Bank to developing countries in the form of monetary grants, loans at low interest rates, in kind, or a combination of these is called aid. Aid can also refer to assistance of any type rendered to benefit some group or individual.
Loyalty	Marketers tend to define customer loyalty as making repeat purchases. Some argue that it should be defined attitudinally as a strongly positive feeling about the brand.
Hierarchy	A system of grouping people in an organization according to rank from the top down in which all subordinate managers must report to one person is called a hierarchy.
Service	Service refers to a "non tangible product" that is not embodied in a physical good and that typically effects some change in another product, person, or institution. Contrasts with good.
Gain	In finance, gain is a profit or an increase in value of an investment such as a stock or bond. Gain is calculated by fair market value or the proceeds from the sale of the investment minus the sum of the purchase price and all costs associated with it.
Economic system	Economic system refers to a particular set of institutional arrangements and a coordinating mechanism for solving the economizing problem; a method of organizing an economy, of which the market system and the command system are the two general types.
Welfare	Welfare refers to the economic well being of an individual, group, or economy. For individuals, it is conceptualized by a utility function. For groups, including countries and the world, it is a tricky philosophical concept, since individuals fare differently.
Accommodation	Accommodation is a term used to describe a delivery of nonconforming goods meant as a partial performance of a contract for the sale of goods, where a full performance is not possible.
Interest	In finance and economics, interest is the price paid by a borrower for the use of a lender's money. In other words, interest is the amount of paid to "rent" money for a period of time.
Economic union	A common market with the added feature that additional policies -- monetary, fiscal, welfare -- are also harmonized across the member countries is an economic union.
Union	A worker association that bargains with employers over wages and working conditions is called a union.
Transnational	Transnational focuses on the heightened interconnectivity between people all around the world and the loosening of boundaries between countries.
Profit	Profit refers to the return to the resource entrepreneurial ability; total revenue minus total cost.
Market	A market is, as defined in economics, a social arrangement that allows buyers and sellers to discover information and carry out a voluntary exchange of goods or services.
Compromise	Compromise occurs when the interaction is moderately important to meeting goals and the goals are neither completely compatible nor completely incompatible.
Management	Management characterizes the process of leading and directing all or part of an organization, often a business, through the deployment and manipulation of resources. Early twentieth-century management writer Mary Parker Follett defined management as "the art of getting things done through people."

Go to **Cram101.com** for the Practice Tests for this Chapter.

Chapter 17. INTERNATIONAL ORGANIZATION IN RETROSPECT AND PROSPECT

Chapter 17. INTERNATIONAL ORGANIZATION IN RETROSPECT AND PROSPECT

Tariff	A tax imposed by a nation on an imported good is called a tariff.
United Nations	An international organization created by multilateral treaty in 1945 to promote social and economic cooperation among nations and to protect human rights is the United Nations.
Economic resources	Economic resources refers to the land, labor, capital, and entrepreneurial ability that are used in the production of goods and services; productive agents; factors of production.
Promotion	Promotion refers to all the techniques sellers use to motivate people to buy products or services. An attempt by marketers to inform people about products and to persuade them to participate in an exchange.
Developing country	Developing country refers to a country whose per capita income is low by world standards. Same as LDC. As usually used, it does not necessarily connote that the country's income is rising.
Technology	The body of knowledge and techniques that can be used to combine economic resources to produce goods and services is called technology.
Interdependence	The extent to which departments depend on each other for resources or materials to accomplish their tasks is referred to as interdependence.
Escalation	Regarding the structure of tariffs. In the context of a trade war, escalation refers to the increase in tariffs that occurs as countries retaliate again and again.
Wage	The payment for the service of a unit of labor, per unit time. In trade theory, it is the only payment to labor, usually unskilled labor. In empirical work, wage data may exclude other compenzation, which must be added to get the total cost of employment.
Charter	Charter refers to an instrument or authority from the sovereign power bestowing the right or power to do business under the corporate form of organization. Also, the organic law of a city or town, and representing a portion of the statute law of the state.
Security	Security refers to a claim on the borrower future income that is sold by the borrower to the lender. A security is a type of transferable interest representing financial value.
Balance	In banking and accountancy, the outstanding balance is the amount of money owned, (or due), that remains in a deposit account (or a loan account) at a given date, after all past remittances, payments and withdrawal have been accounted for. It can be positive (then, in the balance sheet of a firm, it is an asset) or negative (a liability).
Sovereignty	A country or region's power and ability to rule itself and manage its own affairs. Some feel that membership in international organizations such as the WTO is a threat to their sovereignty.
Prerogative	Prerogative refers to a special power, privilege, or immunity, usually used in reference to an official or his office.
Policy	Similar to a script in that a policy can be a less than completely rational decision-making method. Involves the use of a pre-existing set of decision steps for any problem that presents itself.
Budget	Budget refers to an account, usually for a year, of the planned expenditures and the expected receipts of an entity. For a government, the receipts are tax revenues.
Utility	Utility refers to the want-satisfying power of a good or service; the satisfaction or pleasure a consumer obtains from the consumption of a good or service.
Channel	Channel, in communications (sometimes called communications channel), refers to the medium used to convey information from a sender (or transmitter) to a receiver.
Controlling	A management function that involves determining whether or not an organization is progressing

Go to **Cram101.com** for the Practice Tests for this Chapter.

Chapter 17. INTERNATIONAL ORGANIZATION IN RETROSPECT AND PROSPECT

Chapter 17. INTERNATIONAL ORGANIZATION IN RETROSPECT AND PROSPECT

	toward its goals and objectives, and taking corrective action if it is not is called controlling.
International law	Law that governs affairs between nations and that regulates transactions between individuals and businesses of different countries is an international law.
Treaties	The first source of international law, consisting of agreements or contracts between two or more nations that are formally signed by an authorized representative and ratified by the supreme power of each nation are called treaties.
Comprehensive	A comprehensive refers to a layout accurate in size, color, scheme, and other necessary details to show how a final ad will look. For presentation only, never for reproduction.
Jurisdiction	The power of a court to hear and decide a case is called jurisdiction. It is the practical authority granted to a formally constituted body or to a person to deal with and make pronouncements on legal matters and, by implication, to administer justice within a defined area of responsibility.
Authority	Authority in agency law, refers to an agent's ability to affect his principal's legal relations with third parties. Also used to refer to an actor's legal power or ability to do something. In addition, sometimes used to refer to a statute, case, or other legal source that justifies a particular result.
Adoption	In corporation law, a corporation's acceptance of a pre-incorporation contract by action of its board of directors, by which the corporation becomes liable on the contract, is referred to as adoption.
Negotiation	Negotiation is the process whereby interested parties resolve disputes, agree upon courses of action, bargain for individual or collective advantage, and/or attempt to craft outcomes which serve their mutual interests.
Intermediate range	The upward sloping segment of the aggregate supply curve lying between the horizontal range and the vertical range is called intermediate range.
Foundation	A Foundation is a type of philanthropic organization set up by either individuals or institutions as a legal entity (either as a corporation or trust) with the purpose of distributing grants to support causes in line with the goals of the foundation.
Personnel	A collective term for all of the employees of an organization. Personnel is also commonly used to refer to the personnel management function or the organizational unit responsible for administering personnel programs.
Corporation	A legal entity chartered by a state or the Federal government that is distinct and separate from the individuals who own it is a corporation. This separation gives the corporation unique powers which other legal entities lack.
Multinational corporations	Firms that own production facilities in two or more countries and produce and sell their products globally are referred to as multinational corporations.
Multinational corporation	An organization that manufactures and markets products in many different countries and has multinational stock ownership and multinational management is referred to as multinational corporation.
Inputs	The inputs used by a firm or an economy are the labor, raw materials, electricity and other resources it uses to produce its outputs.
Acceleration	Acceleration refers to the shortening of the time for the performance of a contract or the payment of a note by the operation of some provision in the contract or note itself.
Cooperative	A business owned and controlled by the people who use it, producers, consumers, or workers with similar needs who pool their resources for mutual gain is called cooperative.

Go to Cram101.com for the Practice Tests for this Chapter.

Chapter 17. INTERNATIONAL ORGANIZATION IN RETROSPECT AND PROSPECT

Chapter 17. INTERNATIONAL ORGANIZATION IN RETROSPECT AND PROSPECT

Economic problem	Economic problem refers to how to determine the use of scarce resources among competing uses. Because resources are scarce, the economy must choose what products to produce; how these products are to be produced: and for whom.
Instrument	Instrument refers to an economic variable that is controlled by policy makers and can be used to influence other variables, called targets. Examples are monetary and fiscal policies used to achieve external and internal balance.
Integration	Economic integration refers to reducing barriers among countries to transactions and to movements of goods, capital, and labor, including harmonization of laws, regulations, and standards. Integrated markets theoretically function as a unified market.
Beneficiary	The person for whose benefit an insurance policy, trust, will, or contract is established is a beneficiary. In the case of a contract, the beneficiary is called a third-party beneficiary.
Aggregation	Aggregation refers to the combining of two or more things into a single category. Data on international trade necessarily aggregate goods and services into manageable groups.
Context	The effect of the background under which a message often takes on more and richer meaning is a context. Context is especially important in cross-cultural interactions because some cultures are said to be high context or low context.
Trend	Trend refers to the long-term movement of an economic variable, such as its average rate of increase or decrease over enough years to encompass several business cycles.
A share	In finance the term A share has two distinct meanings, both relating to securities. The first is a designation for a 'class' of common or preferred stock. A share of common or preferred stock typically has enhanced voting rights or other benefits compared to the other forms of shares that may have been created. The equity structure, or how many types of shares are offered, is determined by the corporate charter.
Status quo	Status quo is a Latin term meaning the present, current, existing state of affairs.

Chapter 17. INTERNATIONAL ORGANIZATION IN RETROSPECT AND PROSPECT

Printed in the United States
73334LV00002B/95